SEEING
IS
BELIEVING!

SEEING IS BELIEVING!

Youth Talks for Every Occasion

Todd Outcalt

Abingdon Press
Nashville

SEEING IS BELIEVING!
100 YOUTH TALKS FOR EVERY OCCASION

This book is printed on acid-free, recycled paper.

Library of Congress Cataloging-in-Publication Data

   Outcalt, Todd.
      Seeing is believing! : 100 youth talks for every occasion / Todd Outcalt.
      p. cm.
      Includes index.
      ISBN 0-687-07182-8 (pbk. : alk. paper)
      1. Youth sermons. 2. Sermons, American. I. Title.
   BV4310.098 1998
   268'.433—dc21   98-25979
                                                CIP

Scripture quotations in this publication are from the Contemporary English Version Bible. Copyright © American Bible Society, 1995. Used by permission.

To the youth group of University Heights United Methodist Church
good friends, joyous memories

98 99 00 01 02 03 04 05 06 07—10 9 8 7 6 5 3 2 1

MANUFACTURED IN THE UNITED STATES OF AMERICA

CONTENTS

ACKNOWLEDGMENTS

Writing this book of youth talks has exercised my memory as well as my creativity. Many of these talks were given at youth meetings and retreats, on mission trips, and before sporting events. I am grateful for all of the teenagers and the youth workers who have crossed paths with me over the years. This collection of talks is as much yours as mine.

I also thank my editor, Eric Skinner, and the fine people at Abingdon Press who have demonstrated great faith in allowing me to write this series of books. And to my wife and children, I am grateful for your love and patience during the process of committing these words to the line of the *Essentials for Christian Youth*. You have my undying love and gratitude.

USING YOUTH TALKS WITH TEENAGERS

Some years ago, at the beginning of my ministry, I had organized a weekend retreat for teenagers, complete with recreation, free time, and, of course, the obligatory worship and learning sessions. As the weekend progressed and the teenagers became increasingly reluctant to learn anything, I asked one of the teenagers for some feedback.

"It would help if you had something to show as well as tell," was the response. As I thought about it, the observation made sense. Mere talk can become dry and boring. But showing has a way of adding excitement. This is especially true when one is addressing teenagers.

Teenagers are tuned in to the visible. They want to see as well as hear and touch. They want to know and learn through experience.

This emphasis on sight can be a challenge to youth leaders when it comes to communication. Teenagers tend to turn off the moment an adult wants to "get serious." It's as if they can feel a sermon coming on and they don't want to hear it.

Preparing good youth talks is one way to address teens, to speak their language, and to communicate a message effectively. Holding an object in hand—particularly an object that is of interest to teen culture—serves as a kind of "hook." Teenagers look at an electronic pager and they will naturally want to hear what a leader says about it. A leader who takes out a tube of zit medication is bound to command a captive audience.

The talks in this book have been used at many youth meetings over the years. But they are only a beginning point for the creative youth leader. These talks are mere nuggets, small seeds that can be transformed into longer discussions, conversations, and study opportunities. The talks can be used as lessons, quick conversation starters, or brief devotionals, which can be given at athletic events, before recreation times, or on mission trips.

In addition to these possibilities, the talks included in SEEING IS BELIEVING! provide the youth leader with a diversity of presentation styles: stories, essays, and more straightforward approaches to teaching. Again, these can be presented as they are found in the book or can serve merely as a starting point for a particular theme, Scripture reference, or youth event.

Youth leaders also are encouraged to involve teenagers in the talks, either by way of engaging youth in discussion or through inviting the youth to present the talks themselves. With a bit of practice, youth could readily use these talks to speak to their peers.

Brief forms of communication can be used effectively in youth ministry, particularly if talks are given at opportune times and situations. SEEING IS BELIEVING! was designed to serve as a ready guide for the busy youth leader who finds it difficult to prepare talks or who desires a volume that can address a given situation or theme with a quick turn of a page.

As I have thought about that early retreat over the years, I've come to realize that great talks don't have to be lengthy or penetrating to be insightful and helpful to teenagers. All youth want from us is honesty and love. I think these talks contain generous helpings of both. And I hope they can touch the heart of young people as well as the mind.

Chapter One

CROWDBREAKER YOUTH TALKS

#1: BIRTHDAY CANDLE CELEBRATION

Themes: SELF-ESTEEM, INDIVIDUALITY

Scripture: Keep your Creator in mind while you are young! (Ecclesiastes 12:1)

Preparation: a box of birthday candles, matches

Here's the Talk

How many of you can remember your first birthday? second? third? fourth? What is the earliest memory you have of a birthday? Birthdays are special because they say something about who we are. When each of us was born, the complexity of the world was changed in some small way. The world is not the same place because each of us has been born. We exist. And so we have each made a difference simply by virtue of that fact alone.

Take a moment to consider the friends who are with you today. Each one is unique. We have different birthdays, are different ages, have different looks and personalities. And yet we have found ourselves together in this place at this time. That alone is a cause for celebration. You make a difference—and if you were not here tonight, somehow our time together would be changed. (*Allow each person to take a candle from the box.*)

Take a moment to light the candle of a friend. Give thanks for the fact that each one of us counts. We all make a difference. And the glowing of our individual candles burns even brighter when we are together.

#2: HOW FEET IT IS

Theme: **APPRECIATION**

Scripture: Every time I remember you, I thank my God. And whenever I mention you in my prayers, it makes me happy. (Philippians 1:3-4)

Preparation: butcher paper and markers

Here's the Talk

I'd like for everyone to find a partner. Take turns standing on the butcher paper, and trace around your partner's shoes. (*Allow time for everyone to do this.*)

Now stand back for a moment and look at all the different sizes of shoes we all wear. Some of us have wide feet, others have narrow. Some of us have big feet, others small. Perhaps some of us even have to wear special types of shoes. Even so, we would never choose a friend based upon the size of his or her feet. No. We grow to appreciate each other because of our individual personalities, our appearances, our smiles, our talents.

As we begin our group today, it is important for us to appreciate each other. We need to support each other as much as possible. For we are all unique—just as our footprints are unique. Our differences are important to God, because God has created us that way.

Today take a few moments to look at the other people in our group. Think about the individual gifts each one possesses. We can pray for each other and give thanks to God whenever we think about each other. Let's do that right now by making a circle and giving thanks for all the wonderful friends we have in our group.

#3: Amazing Zits

Theme: GRACE

Scripture: Christ did this, so that he would have a glorious and holy church, without faults or spots or wrinkles or any other flaws. (Ephesians 5:27)

Preparation: a tube of acne medication

Here's the Talk

I hold in my hand a tube of zit medicine! This tube of gunk promises to clear up blemishes, dry the skin, and generally make us more beautiful or handsome. The tube has many active ingredients that have been scientifically tested on lab rats. And if this medicine can beautify a rodent, imagine what it can do for us!

It's funny, isn't it—how all of us want to look perfect? We don't want to have blemishes, even though we know that zits are just a part of adolescence. But, even though we think the outside is what is most important, God is looking on the inside. We don't have to be perfect to please God. Jesus has done that for us. This is called grace. Jesus died so we could be without blemish on the inside.

And if God has shown us this much grace, why shouldn't we be gracious to each other? Let's remind each other that we are forgiven people, not perfect people. Let's form a circle and give each other a living reminder that we are each very special to God.

(Form a circle. Then take turns applying a small dab of the acne medicine to the forehead of a friend seated next to you. As you apply the medicine say, "In the name of Christ, you are forgiven.")

#4: JAWBREAKER BASICS

Theme: PATIENCE

Scripture: Love is kind and patient. (1 Corinthians 13:4)

Preparation: jawbreakers for everyone

Here's the Talk

(Pass out the jawbreakers and issue a challenge: no one can bite the jawbreaker until the meeting is over.)

Jawbreakers have been around for a long time. But many people don't like them. I suppose that is because it takes so long to finish a jawbreaker. Finishing a jawbreaker without biting it takes patience. We don't ever think we are going to get to the center.

Sometimes we live like we are eating a jawbreaker. We want things to happen much faster than is possible. We get impatient and want to bite off more than we can chew. We miss a lot of life that way.

But love is always patient. And God's love is the most patient love of all. God doesn't get upset when we make mistakes, when we do things too quickly. Instead, God loves us all the more and wants to teach us how to slow down and take every step of life in its proper time. There is a proper time for everything in your future and mine, and we don't need to rush. Tomorrow is God's gift to us. God wants us to enjoy the adventure of learning as we go.

Perhaps some of you have felt rushed to do things too quickly or at the wrong time. Maybe you have rushed into a relationship or sex. Maybe you have taken a bad job or have decided that school is of no use to your future. But God wants you to be patient. God would not have you rush too quickly into life. Learn how to love by being patient with yourself and others. Don't expect someone else to give more than he or she is willing or able to give. Don't let someone else rush you. Think about these things as you enjoy your jawbreaker. And try not to bite it until you get to the center!

#5: WHAT'S IN A NAME?

Theme: FRIENDSHIP

Scripture: A good reputation and respect are worth much more than silver and gold. (Proverbs 22:1)

Preparation a book of baby names with their meanings

Here's the Talk

Think how chaotic the world would be if no one had names. How would we talk to, and about, each other? How would we know if someone was trying to speak to us? How could we give instructions, assistance, or pass along information? Names are important. And each of us has one.

Let's take a few moments to form a circle; then we will each say our full names. As we say our names, I will look up each person's first name in this baby book and tell the group what the name means. (*Allow time for this activity*.)

What person in our group do you think has the prettiest name? Who has the most meaningful name? The most symbolic? Whose name surprises you? Whose name most befits his or her personality?

In the Book of Proverbs we are told that it is better to be respected than to have great wealth. We know this is true. Each of us wants to be liked, loved, and appreciated. But this type of respect is never something we are born with. We have to earn respect and trust by showing other people that we have character and deep values.

Think about your name for a moment. Think about the name of the person standing next to you. Now turn and tell a friend why you respect him or her.

#6: PICTURE PERFECT

Themes: SELF-ESTEEM, GOD'S GRACE

Scripture: You are like light for the whole world. (Matthew 5:14)

Preparation: a camera with film

Here's the Talk

(Begin the talk by inviting everyone to pose for a group picture.)

From time to time I meet people who do not like to get their pictures taken. Some people think a photograph makes them look too short, too silly, or too thin. Other people are convinced that they should not have their picture taken because it makes them look too young or too old. Maybe you know someone like this.

However, what we see on the outside does not truly represent who we are. A photograph only shows what we look like from the skin out! But a picture doesn't tell us much about who we are on the inside.

Long ago, Jesus told people, "You are like light for the whole world." Have you ever wondered what he might have meant by those words? I think Jesus was trying to tell people that everyone has something to offer the kingdom of God. Each of us can be light to someone else. We can help show the way or point the way to God. Jesus looked at each person and saw something special inside that individual. He looks at you and me the same way—he sees what is on the inside.

Now we are going to get our picture taken as a group. Later I will put the photo on the wall. But when you look at your own face in the photo, don't think about what you look like on the outside. Think about what you are on the inside; think about what you have to give to others; think about how special you are to God. *(Close by taking a group photo.)*

#7: TUNING IN

Theme: ANTICIPATION

Scripture: Ask, and you will receive. Search, and you will find. Knock, and the door will be opened for you. (Matthew 7:7)

Preparation: a radio

Here's the Talk

Even though radio was invented long before television, radio is still a very influential form of communication in our world. (*Hold up the radio and "tune in" to several local stations; allow the teens to listen for a minute.*)

What did you hear when I was tuning in to the various stations? (*commercials, music, advertising, humor*)

Every time we gather as a youth group, we are asked to tune out our worries, cares, and prejudices and tune in to God's way. Every youth meeting will be an opportunity to learn, grow, and experience something new in our faith. Jesus once told the disciples, "Knock, and the door will be opened for you." When you and I seek God, God will always provide a message or a path for us. We may have to keep tuning in over a period of time to get on God's wavelength, but in time God's way will become clear to us.

I hope you look forward to youth meetings as much as I do. When we are learning together and growing together, great things happen—to all of us.

#8: Getting to Know Ya

Themes: **Friendship, Community**

Scripture: All the Lord's followers often met together, and they shared everything they had. (Acts 2:44)

Preparation: a balloon

Here's the Talk

(Invite the teenagers to form two groups. Blow up a balloon, tie the end so the air won't leak out, and give the balloon to one group.)

Being part of a church youth group is special because we become a family of God when we learn to care about each other. One of the ways we learn to care for each other is through listening. Today as we begin our meeting, I'd like for us to listen to each other. We will do this by having some fun with a balloon. One group will bat the balloon to the other group. When the balloon touches someone in the group, he or she must then respond to the situation that I will read aloud. Afterwards, this person will bat the balloon to the other group, and we will repeat the process until everyone has responded to a situation.

(After the balloon has been batted and touches someone, use the list below—or make up your own—to help the teens get to know each other better.)

- Tell us about your most embarrassing moment.
- Tell us about your most memorable vacation.
- Tell us about your family.
- Tell us what you hope to be when you grow up.
- Tell us about your greatest aspiration in life.
- Tell us where you hope to live and why.
- Tell us about your dream home.

#9: VIDEO VALUATION

Themes: THANKFULNESS, GRATITUDE

Scripture: Our God, we thank you for being so near to us!
(Psalm 75:1)

Preparation: a video camera, tape, video cassette player, and
television

Here's the Talk

(Post a volunteer near the door to videotape the youth as they walk in. Ask each teenager, "What has God done for you this week?" Record the responses. Gather the group around the television and begin the meeting.)

Each day of our lives God does great things for us. Some of these "great things" go unnoticed—such as life itself, or family or friendships. Other blessings come to us in such a way that we know that God has given them—such as a moment or expression of love, a new job, or a peaceful day of rest. I hope each of you experienced many blessings this week and can give thanks to God. Even the humorous moments of life are worth celebrating. Let's see what we have to celebrate as a youth group this week. *(Play the videotape—five minutes will be more than enough—and then ask the teenagers to respond to the following questions.)*

- What joys did you hear expressed from members of our group?
- How does watching this tape make you more thankful?

(Close with prayer.)

#10: Making the Grade

Themes: GROWTH, SUPPORT, GOD'S GRACE

Scripture: Love should always make us tell the truth. Then we will grow in every way and be more like Christ, the head of the body. (Ephesians 4:15)

Preparation: an old report card

Here's the Talk

In school we get used to getting a report card at the end of each term. The report card supposedly tells us how well we have performed in certain subjects or classes. Sometimes our grades are what we expected. Other times they might exceed or fall below what we had hoped. Either way, the specter of the report card always looms over us—as if we have to measure up to a standard that is demanded of us.

For a moment, forget about all the demands others place on us and that we place on ourselves. Growing in Christ and trying to live up to his standard is much different than trying to make a good grade.

One reason is that, when we are in Christ, we know others who will help encourage us. Remember, we are never alone. We are a community of faith, not just individuals who have faith. We don't always have to make the grade on our own; we can do it together.

Growing in Christ is different than trying to make a good grade. We know that, when we fail, God has promised grace and mercy. You see, you and I have already been given an "A" on our report cards. God gave us an "A" the day we were born. We were given an "A" today. We will be given an "A" tomorrow. Why? Because of what Jesus has already done for us.

Now let's give thanks for what God has already done for us. We've already made the grade because of God's grace. What we do with our lives each day shows our gratitude for this fact.

(Close with prayer.)

#11: LIVING YOUR DIPLOMA

Themes: FAMILY, PARENTS, GOD'S BLESSINGS

Scripture: Children, you belong to the Lord, and you do the right thing when you obey your parents. (Ephesians 6:1)

Preparation: a high school or college diploma

Here's the Talk

DeAnna and Ronda Miller grew up in a small town in Georgia, a close-knit African American community where poverty was the norm. Lucille Miller, their mother, worked two and sometimes three jobs in order to make ends meet. In spite of the fact that their home had no indoor plumbing and circumstances were harsh, DeAnna became salutatorian of her class, and Ronda became one of the few black valedictorians in the history of Ludowici High School in Long County, Georgia.

DeAnna is a pre-med biology major at Benedict College in South Carolina; Ronda majors in psychology at Spelman College in Atlanta. Behind their accomplishments is their faith, hard work, and a deep love for their mother, who stood by them and instilled in them a love of learning and a positive self-esteem.

Like DeAnna and Ronda, you and I are blessed with family and friends who care about us. Take time in this worship experience to give thanks for your parents. A diploma is a great accomplishment in life, but God asks us to honor our father and mother all the days of our lives. This is a lifetime goal and is one of the highest expressions of our love for God. Love is a great power. The love of our parents can give us far more than we will ever know.

(Close with prayer or by lighting candles in honor of parents.)

#12: THE LEAKY UMBRELLA

Themes: **FORGIVENESS, SIN**

Scripture: You were saved by faith in God, who treats us much better than we deserve. This is God's gift to you, and not anything you have done on your own. (Ephesians 2:8)

Preparation: an umbrella with holes in it

Here's the Talk

(Begin by opening up the umbrella, showing the holes.)

If I were to go out in the rain today, you can see that I would get very wet. An umbrella with holes doesn't do much good when it is raining.

Your life and mine are like that, too. We want to be perfect, but we know that there are places in our lives where hate, apathy, jealousy, and pride slip through. We want to keep the bad out—those things we call sins—but somehow, they always slip in. It's tough following Jesus when we can't seem to live up to his standards.

But God has made a way for us. The Bible tells us that salvation is a gift from God. Salvation is not something we earn or deserve. Forgiveness comes by God's grace through faith—a faith grounded not in ourselves, but in Jesus, who is our shield and protector.

Today, give thanks to God for the gift of salvation, the gift of forgiveness in Jesus. You and I have many places where sin creeps into our lives, but God is more powerful than them all.

(Close with prayer or invite the youth to offer signs of God's forgiveness and peace to each other.)

#13: SOUL FOOD

Themes: GOD'S STRENGTH, THE SCRIPTURES

Scripture: Jesus answered, "The Scriptures say: 'No one can live only on food. People need every word that God has spoken.' " (Matthew 4:4)

Preparation: a variety of snack foods

Here's the Talk

How many of you like to eat junk food? We all do, because it tastes good. But the problem with junk food is that it doesn't satisfy the body's nutritional needs. That's why we feel hungry again soon after we fill up with it. These foods don't satisfy us for very long.

In the Gospel of Matthew, one temptation Jesus endured was the temptation to turn stones into bread. He had fasted for many days, and he was hungry. A little bread would hit the spot. But Jesus resisted this temptation. He knew that physical sustenance is only part of what we need. In addition to food and water, we also need spiritual nourishment.

That is what worship is all about. When we pause to remember that God is our Creator and provider, we are drawn into God's strength and not our own. Worship calls us beyond ourselves to that quiet place of the heart where God speaks to us, calls us, and assures us that we are God's.

Let's take these moments to worship God today. Let's put aside things that do not satisfy us and concentrate only on loving God. In these moments we can truly find the bread of life.

(*Close with moments of Scripture reading, prayer, testimonies of faith, or other acts of worship.*)

#14: BABY BLANKET BINGO

Themes: COMFORT, ASSURANCE

Scripture: Our God has said: "Encourage my people! Give them comfort." (Isaiah 40:1)

Preparation: a tattered baby blanket

Here's the Talk

How many of you remember having a favorite blanket when you were little? Why was this blanket important to you? (*Allow the teenagers to offer answers.*)

No doubt your favorite blanket was a source of comfort when you were a baby. We outgrow our need for our favorite blanket, but we never outgrow our longing and desire to be comforted. The Scriptures attest to the fact that God is our comforter. God is the one who is able to lift us up when we are feeling down, who supports us when we are in pain, sorrow, or loneliness. We all need God's comfort.

(*Read the Scripture text, then ask the following questions.*)

• When do you most need God's comfort?
• How do you sense the comfort of God?

As I pass the blanket around, take a moment to recognize those times in your life when God has been especially near to you. Let the blanket be a reminder that God's comfort is never far away.

#15: THE GAME OF LIFE

Themes: OPPORTUNITIES, TRUST

Scripture: I came so that everyone would have life, and have it in its fullest. (John 10:10)

Preparation: a board game

Here's the Talk

(Set up a board game where everyone can view it easily. Move a few of the pieces around the board as you begin the talk.)

Once there was a man who hated his circumstances and decided to look for heaven. One evening, when his family was asleep, he left the house and began to walk. After three days he grew weary and decided to stop for a bit of sleep. Taking off his shoes, he pointed them in the direction he had been traveling, so that upon awakening the next morning he could continue in the right direction.

While he slept, someone came along and moved the man's shoes, pointing them in the opposite direction. When the man awakened, he put on his shoes and started off again, not realizing he was backtracking every step of the way. Three days later he came upon a village, noting that it looked vaguely familiar. Entering the village, he saw a street that looked like the one he used to live on. He knocked on the front door of a house that resembled the one he had left behind and was greeted by a woman and children who looked much like his family. He settled there, thinking that he was in heaven, and lived happily until the end of his days.*

Like the man in this story, you and I often search for heaven in all the wrong places, thinking that life will be better if we live somewhere else, make new friends, or have a new job. But we overlook the fact that, with God's help, we can make an abundant life right where we are. We don't need to move through life without any goals, as if we were merely playing pieces on a game board. Jesus said he came to give us an abundant life, and with God's help we can begin living that life right now.

* A variation of this rabbinical teaching is used in Youth Talk #27, which is related to retreats.

#16: SUGAR AND SPICE AND EVERYTHING NICE

Themes: **LOVE, PATIENCE**

Scripture: Love is kind and patient. (1 Corinthians 13:4)

Preparation: a package of sugar

Here's the Talk

Jesus once said, "You are like salt for everyone on earth." Of course, this is a metaphorical way of saying, "You can make everything better." But if Jesus were to give us a metaphor that we could understand more readily in our culture, perhaps he would say we should be like sugar. Sugar is a part of most foods we enjoy—in fact, most of us cannot imagine a world without soft drinks, chocolate, and tasty desserts. Sugar is sweet and tasty, and most people crave it in one form or another.

Have you ever stopped to think how the world would be different if each of us tried to sweeten the world around us? A kind word or a loving action could sweeten. People might even take note of our sweetness and want to try some, too.

Love is kind and patient. That's what our Scripture says. Kindness and patience go a long way in making the world a better place. And, like sugar, it doesn't cost much to be nice to someone. It doesn't cost much to lend a helping hand.

Let's demonstrate our worship of God by going forth to spread a little sweetness into other people's lives. Let's do it at school, at home, and when we go to work. Be kind. Be patient. And that sugar will go a long way toward making everything nicer.

#17: MY PRAYER PAGER

Themes: PRAYER, DEVOTION

Scripture: When you pray, go into a room alone and close the door. Pray to your Father in private. He knows what is done in private, and he will reward you. (Matthew 6:6)

Preparation: an electronic pager or beeper

Here's the Talk

(This talk can be used most effectively as an introduction to a time of prayer.)

How many of you own electronic pagers? Why is it necessary or important to have a pager? (*Allow the youth to give answers.*)

Pagers are, in essence, devices that keep us in touch with others. We have them so we will never be out of touch with family, friends, or employers. We are always accessible. Others can always reach us.

Did you know that God has a pager, too? That's right. We can get in touch with God any time we want. This pager is prayer. And Jesus talked about prayer a lot. In fact, he told his disciples to pray often, to pray in private, and to pray each day. And this was long before anyone ever dreamed of wearing a beeper. All we have to do to communicate with God is focus our attention on the Creator. God is listening. All we have to do is tune in.

Prayer does not have to be complex to be a form of communication with God. We can meditate or speak aloud, write words or whisper them, reach out with our feelings, or just be still and wait for the peace of God. Let's take a few moments today to practice with our prayer pagers. Perhaps you could find a quiet place right now, in silence, as we lift our needs to God.

#18: HEAVENLY MUSIC

Themes: MUSIC, JOY, CELEBRATION

Scripture: Shout praises to the LORD! Sing him a new song of praise. (Psalm 149:1)

Preparation: an assortment of musical instruments

Here's the Talk

(Before the talk, pass out a few instruments. These can be simple ones such as harmonicas, kazoos, wood blocks, bongo drums, and such.)

Close your eyes for a moment. Try to imagine what the world would be like without music. What would the world sound like? How would it be different? What would take the place of music?

Now open your eyes. Listen. Play one of the instruments. *(Allow the teenagers to play the various instruments for a few seconds.)* As you can hear, music is much different than just playing a hodgepodge of notes and rhythms. Everything has to work together—rhythm, melody, treble, and bass—in order for instruments to truly make music.

That's how it is with us, too. Making heavenly music with our lives involves working together, doing things in cooperation with one another. That's the new song that God desires to hear. That is the true praise of God! When you and I learn to make music in our hearts, that is true worship. When, together, we pray and learn and grow, that is the greatest praise we can ever offer to God.

(Close the worship time with a favorite group song or listen to an upbeat song of praise.)

#19: THE GOOD BOOK

Themes: THE BIBLE, LEARNING

Scripture: Everything in the Scriptures is God's Word. All of it is useful for teaching and helping people and for correcting them and showing them how to live. (2 Timothy 3:16)

Preparation: a high school textbook and a Bible

Here's the Talk

(Present this talk prior to a Scripture reading or other act of worship.)

High school presents many challenges, not the least of which is learning how to study well. Sometimes, textbooks don't help matters (*hold up a textbook*). After all, when you first begin a class, a textbook can look very imposing. There seems to be so much information and so little time to learn it.

The same can hold true for the Bible (*hold up a Bible*). When you first look at the Bible, it looks very difficult. It is thick, has small print, and is often written in language that is difficult to understand. Yet the Bible is the most important book for Christians because we believe it is a living dialogue between God and people.

In this book we can read about every type of human failure, weakness, and sin. Some people call the Bible "the Good Book," because they assume the Bible only speaks of good things. But the Bible actually contains many stories of bloodshed, cruelty, and deception. There are stories of adultery, prostitution, and murder. However, one message runs throughout the Bible: In spite of our sinfulness and failures, God desires us, wants us, and loves us. The Bible is a good book because it tells the story of God's interaction in human history.

There is an old saying: The only Bible we truly own is not the Bible we hold in our hands but the Bible we hold in our hearts. I challenge you to take time each day to read the Bible. In this book you will discover God's love for you. You will find a source of learning that never grows old, outdated, or irrelevant.

#20: FRUITS OF THE SPIRIT

Themes: DISCIPLESHIP, GROWTH

Scripture: God's Spirit makes us loving, happy, peaceful, patient, kind, good, faithful, gentle, and self-controlled. (Galatians 5:22-23)

Preparation: a pad of self-stick notes

Here's the Talk

Saint Francis was a Christian who lived in the 13th century in Italy. It is said that he had such compassion for all of God's creatures that he would often preach to the birds of the air and to the animals of the field. Francis believed that everyone, with God's help, could make a difference in the world. Like self-stick notes, Francis believed each Christian could leave something behind that would demonstrate or communicate God's love. Francis is revered as one of the greatest of all saints because of his compassion. A lovely prayer is attributed to Saint Francis:

> Lord, make me an instrument of thy peace;
> where there is hatred, let me sow love;
> where there is injury, pardon;
> where there is doubt, faith;
> where there is despair, hope;
> where there is darkness, light;
> and where there is sadness, joy.

(Close the talk by saying the prayer of Saint Francis together. Give each teen a self-stick note with one or more of the fruits of the Spirit written on it and ask them to try to live out that fruit of the Spirit in the coming week.)

CHAPTER THREE

RETREAT YOUTH TALKS

#21: WHAT TIME IS IT?

Theme: GROUP BUILDING

Scripture: Everything on earth has its own time and its own season. (Ecclesiastes 3:1)

Preparation: a wristwatch

Here's the Talk

(Begin the retreat by collecting wristwatches from the youth group. Hold up a wristwatch, read the Scripture text, and then begin the talk.)

Almost everything we do in life revolves around time—adhering to a schedule, marking off days on a yearly calendar as the seasons float by, looking forward to certain holidays and events. We might say time is the most important commodity we have in life. People long for more time with family and friends, negotiate for longer vacations, and often are willing to take a salary cut to work fewer hours. Some people even say that time is money.

But everyone needs some time away from the demands of time itself. That is what this retreat is about. Without our watches, we are free to just be ourselves, relax, and enjoy each other's friendship. We don't have to be anywhere or do anything. We can focus our attention on God and truly make the most of a day.

The Scriptures remind us that, someday, each of us will run out of time and we will enter into eternity. Such a thought is impossible for us to grasp, but we can try to make the most of the time we have now. During this retreat, let's pledge to make time for God, to relax and take in God's peace and joy, and to make room in our busy lives for tranquillity and recreation.

#22: UNDERWEAR THEOLOGY

Themes: VALUES, SPIRITUALITY

Scripture: With my whole heart I agree with the Law of God. (Romans 7:22)

Preparation: several styles and brands of underwear

Here's the Talk

(As you proceed with this humorous talk, hold up a different pair of underwear from time to time.)

There is famous children's story about an emperor who was proud and arrogant. He wanted all the people of his kingdom to see how rich and powerful he was. One day, some tricksters came through town and talked the gullible king into buying some fine clothes, the likes of which had never been seen before. They told the king that he was wearing a set of fine garments, which looked invisible but were actually the finest set of clothes ever made. These tricksters told the king that all of the people would see beautiful royal robes of purple and gold. All went well for the emperor and his invisible clothes until one day, during a grand parade through the city, a young boy, in his innocence, called out, "Hey, look! The emperor has no clothes!"

This classic story has many lessons for us. What might some of these be?

(Break into smaller groups and ask each group to read the Scripture text. Ask each group to discuss the lessons that can be learned from the Bible text and the story of the emperor's invisible clothes. This activity is a fun way to end the first day of a retreat and will provide some marvelous and funny insights.)

#23: TOOL TIME

Theme: VISION

Scripture: There are different kinds of spiritual gifts, but they all come from the same Spirit. (1 Corinthians 12:4)

Preparation: a utility box filled with assorted tools

Here's the Talk

(This talk works best on a retreat when the teens are divided into smaller groups for discussion.)

In most homes, a tool box is quite helpful. Tools come in handy in all kinds of situations, especially unexpected ones—like when an electrical wire shorts out or a curtain rod falls down. But having the right tool for the right job is important, too. Unless we have prepared in advance for the unexpected job, a box full of useless tools doesn't help much.

In your small groups, I'd like for you to think for a moment about our youth group. How is our group progressing? How are we growing? What could we do that would make a difference? As you consider these questions, I invite each of you to come up to the utility box and remove a tool that, symbolically, you think could be used to make a difference, that might be the right tool for our group. For example, one of you might choose an adjustable wrench because you believe we need to be more flexible in our programming. Someone else might choose the set of jumper cables because you think our group needs a spark. (*Allow time for the teens to choose their tools.*)

Now, in your groups, I'd like for you to discuss these questions:
- What might our youth group need to focus on in the coming year?
- What "tools" would help us to do this job better?
- What do you consider the most successful and meaningful moments of the past year? (and how can we make them meaningful this year?)

#24: MIRROR, MIRROR, ON THE WALL

Theme: ETERNAL LIFE

Scripture: Now all we can see of God is like a cloudy picture in a mirror. (1 Corinthians 13:12)

Preparation: a cracked mirror

Here's the Talk

In the story of Snow White, the wicked queen is so taken with her own beauty that she asks the magic mirror each day, "Mirror, Mirror, on the wall, who's the fairest of them all?" And, of course, we know the rest of the story.

Long ago, mirrors were not anything like we have today. Most mirrors were pieces of polished metal or brass. Because the surface of the mirror was rarely unblemished or clear, the image reflected there was often wavy or dim. The apostle Paul, in this Scripture passage, says that this present life is like looking into such a mirror (hold up the cracked mirror). The image reflected here is not perfect, it does not provide a true representation of what we will be like.

But the apostle goes on to say that someday we will know the fullness of God face to face. The life that God has prepared for us will be far superior to the life we know now. The eternal life God will give us is far beyond our comprehension. This present life is just a dim reflection of the life to come.

I hope that as you consider God's gift of eternal life you will give thanks. God has prepared an incomparable life to come, for all of us. But you won't be able to look in any mirror to find it.

#25: COMMERCIAL FOR CHRIST

Theme: **EVANGELISM**

Scripture: Things that are seen don't last forever, but things that are not seen are eternal. (2 Corinthians 4:18)

Preparation: a television set (preferably one that does not work)

Here's the Talk

How many of you are suffering from television withdrawal on this retreat? Perhaps you are wondering what you missed on your favorite show or who won the big football game. (*Bring out the television to rousing cheers, but then show the teens that it doesn't work.*)

Oh, well. Even though the television doesn't work, we can still have a commercial. (*For best effect, practice reading this commercial aloud, or, if you prefer, invite one of the youth to read it aloud.*)

> Ladies and gentlemen, I am here to introduce you to the greatest savior of all time. He slices! He dices! He walks on water and calms the winds with a single word! And now, for an unlimited time, he can be yours—absolutely free! That's right, absolutely free, with no obligation to buy anything—ever! He's yours for the asking with this special television offer, or any other time. Jesus comes free with his own reward package and special discount coupon known as the Church. This is no gimmick! This is a once-in-a-lifetime offer! Call in now! And, if you call on him before midnight tonight, he'll throw in—at not extra charge—the assurance of the Holy Spirit. So don't delay! Get on those knees! Send no money now—or ever! Just pray! He's standing by!

(*This "commercial" may be used either as an evangelism moment or as a discussion starter. Follow-up questions could include: How is the message of Jesus most effectively communicated today? Is it right or wrong to market the Christian message? What kind of a commercial would you produce to communicate the message of God's love in Jesus?*)

#26: ALL CREATURES GREAT AND SMALL

Themes: GOD'S CREATION, STEWARDSHIP

Scripture: God looked at what he had done. All of it was very good! (Genesis 1:31)

Preparation: a pet (cat or dog)

Here's the Talk

(Begin this talk by telling a story about your favorite pet.)

Several years ago there was a veterinarian named James Herriot who wrote a series of highly successful books about animals. These books appeal to the many people who own pets or who enjoy reading true stories about animals. Many of his accounts deal with dogs and cats and, of course, their owners.

Part of the appeal of his books was that James Herriot had a way of writing about the wonder of God's world in very simple ways. The creation story in Genesis 1 celebrates all living things, not just people. When God looked upon the creation, God saw that everything was good. God was pleased.

In the early church, animals were often blessed in special ceremonies. People would bring their animals to affirm that these creatures, too, had received the goodness of God. Today, there is a growing awareness that all things are connected in creation. God asked human beings to be caretakers of the earth, to use the earth's resources wisely. This is a part of good stewardship. Each day we have an opportunity to leave our world a little cleaner, a bit brighter than the day before. Let us rejoice in all of God's gifts of creation.

#27: WHAT ARE YOU LOOKING FOR?

Themes: VALUES, FAMILY

Scripture: Your kindness and love will always be with me each day of my life. (Psalm 23:6)

Preparation: a family picture

Here's the Talk

(Place the picture of the family next to you as you tell this story.)

There is a Jewish legend that tells of a man who went in search of heaven. One day he left his wife and children and set out to find the holy city. For three days he traveled, growing more weary with every step. Finally he decided to sleep for a short while. In order to ensure that he would be headed in the right direction when he awakened, the man took off his shoes, sat them in the road, and pointed them in the direction he had been traveling.

While he slept, someone came along and pointed the shoes in the opposite direction. When the man awoke, he put on his shoes and set off again, not realizing that he was heading back in the direction he had come.

Three days later, as it happened, the man noticed that the countryside appeared more and more familiar. "Aha," he said, "I must be getting close to heaven." As he neared a town, the fellow noted that the streets looked familiar also. He saw a house that looked much like the one he had left behind. "Yes, this must be heaven," he told himself.

The man went to the front door, knocked, and was greeted by a woman and children who looked much like the family he had left behind. He went in, lived there, and was happy.*

(If you like, invite the group to discuss these questions: What does this story tell us about values? about heaven? What does this story say about desire?)

---

* A variation of this rabbinical teaching is used in Youth Talk #15, which is related to worship.

#28: ALTARED STATES

Themes: WORSHIP, ADORATION

Scripture: I am the LORD your God. …Do not worship any god except me. (Exodus 20:2-3)

Preparation: a table or other furnishing which can be used as an altar

Here's the Talk

The Book of Exodus tells us about the ancient Israelites and their journey from Egypt. While they were slaves there, God told Moses to lead the people to a new land of plenty, a land of hope. The people did leave, but only after God inflicted Egypt with many plagues. Later, however, when the people were wandering in the wilderness, God gave commandments to Moses, telling the people how to live. One commandment—the first one—says, "Do not worship any god except me."

Although the people rarely kept God's commands, they did believe that God was always with them. Inside a tabernacle, the people carried an altar, a place where sacrifices were made and prayers were heard. This tabernacle was portable: it traveled with the people.

On our retreat, we are away from the usual places we associate with God. But that does not mean that God is not present with us. Rather, God goes wherever we go. And if we like, we can even establish a sacred place together. We could, for example, agree that this table will be our altar during the retreat. We will gather for worship here, and we will circle around the altar for our prayers. You see, we can place ourselves in God's presence anytime, anywhere. For God is always with us.

#29: CANDLE IN THE WIND

Themes: **LIFE'S BREVITY, HOPE**

Scripture: Keep your Creator in mind while you are young!
(Ecclesiastes 12:1)

Preparation: a candle

Here's the Talk

In early September 1997 the world was stunned by the death of two famous people, both very different, but each revered and loved in her own right: Princess Diana and Mother Teresa. Princess Diana had married into the royal family at a young age. But her heart for people who were suffering and hurting compelled her to travel the world, spreading words of comfort and hope. She inspired millions and was loved by people far beyond the boundaries of her native England.

Mother Teresa was not royalty, but she served the poor in a different corner of the world. Taking God's love to Calcutta, one of the poorest cities on Earth, Mother Teresa established the Sisters of Charity movement. Often she held the hands of the dying and offered medical assistance to children and mothers. Her free clinics were supported by millions of people from around the world who wanted to follow her example of love.

At Princess Diana's funeral, Elton John sang a variation of his song, "Candle in the Wind." This song reminds us of the brevity of life. Even the rich and the powerful will die. Even good people like Mother Teresa will grow weary and pass away. But God goes on forever. And so does love, faith, and hope.

Remember your Creator in the days of your youth. Life, even if we live to be a hundred years old, is brief by comparison to God's eternity. Strive to live well, to do your part to make the world richer in God's love and compassion.

#30: BRIDAL SHOWER

Themes: SALVATION, CELEBRATION

Scripture: "Come on! I will show you the one who will be the bride and wife of the Lamb." (Revelation 21:9)

Preparation: a wedding invitation

Here's the Talk

A wedding invitation is one of the most flattering invitations we can ever receive. Think about it. When you receive a wedding invitation, you are being invited to share a sacred moment. A man and woman who love each other invite those whom they love the most—their friends and family—to participate in a ceremony where God is present.

In the wedding ceremony itself, there is a line that says, "By his sacrificial love, Christ gave us the example of husband and wife." Many of you may get married at some time in the future or may attend a wedding, and you will hear these words. They are a reminder that love, by its very nature, is sacrificial. And someday, each one of us will participate in a huge wedding party in the kingdom of God. This party will be like a wedding banquet, complete with a wedding party from all of human history.

We who follow Jesus are often called the bride of Christ in the New Testament. This is a metaphorical way of saying how much Christ loves us. And someday God is going to have a big party to welcome us all to this wedding—we will be with God forever. The invitations have already been sent. Everyone is invited. And there is no greater invitation in all the world.

CHAPTER FOUR

FRIENDSHIP YOUTH TALKS

#31: REEL LIFE

Themes: CARE, RESPECT

Scripture: My dear friends, we must love each other. Love comes from God. (1 John 4:7)

Preparation: a movie ticket stub

Here's the Talk

At the Academy Award ceremonies for 1997 there was a short documentary which won best picture in that category. The movie, *Breathing Lessons: The Life and Work of Mark O'Brien*, chronicles the story of Mark O'Brien, who since 1955 has spent every day of his life inside of an iron lung—a 640-pound vacuum chamber that sends air into his lungs. Mark was paralyzed by polio when he was a boy and since that time has been forced to make a life for himself inside a tiny apartment in California.

One day Mark met Jessica Yu, a filmmaker who decided to make a movie of Mark's life. Their friendship, mutual trust, and respect resulted in the award-winning movie. Mark, a writer, spends much of his time each day holding a twelve-inch stick in his mouth as he pecks at a computer keyboard secured above his head. Mark writes essays and poems about his life and serves as an advocate for other people with physical disabilities. Mark's unlikely friendship with Jessica has given hope to many hurting people.

#32: MUSICAL FRIENDS

Themes: HOPE, THE ENVIRONMENT

Scripture: Dear friend, don't copy the evil deeds of others!
Follow the example of people who do kind deeds.
(3 John 11)

Preparation: a CD player

Here's the Talk

When Ocean Robbins and Ryan Eliason met at a summer camp in California, they were just teenagers. But both shared a common dream of making a difference for the environment. Robbins, who was fifteen, and Eliason, who was seventeen, decided to found an organization called YES! (Youth for Environmental Sanity!). Robbins and Eliason put together several comic skits, formed a rock band, and produced their own videos, which have been presented to more than a half million teens in thirty-eight states.

Their music presentations have inspired other teenagers to get involved with environmental issues. Although their music will not be heard on any CD or radio, several big name singers and performers have backed their efforts with time and donations of money.

Robbins and Eliason's friendship resulted in more than $100,000 being raised for environmental needs their first year. Since that time, YES! has sponsored several summer camps for teenagers who are interested in learning more about the environment and what can be done to make a difference.

Consider the friendships you cherish right now. How might God be leading you, as friends, to bring hope and encouragement to others? Together, there is no limit to what you can do.

#33: PULP FICTION

Themes: SINCERITY, TRUTHFULNESS, HONESTY

Scripture: We are part of the same body. Stop lying and start telling each other the truth. (Ephesians 4:25)

Preparation: a popular tabloid magazine

Here's the Talk

Most people would agree that any meaningful friendship must be built on honesty and trust. If friends cannot be truthful with each other, there is little chance that a friendship will blossom and stand the test of time.

As we all know, there are many publications that are built around gossip and half truths. Many people enjoy reading gossip magazines, because there is a kind of enjoyment in reading bad things about others instead of good things. But eventually, when we read only bad things about others, even the good things seem too good to be true.

When friends are not truthful with each other or seek to spread a harmful rumor about another person, this will only lead to misunderstandings and mistrust. In Jesus' day, there were many rumors going around about him, but Jesus was always open with his disciples about how he was feeling. He always reassured them of the truth and of his unwavering love for them. This is the mark of true friendship. And it is the friendship that Jesus has asked us to have with each other.

#34: FRESH STARTS

Theme: **FORGIVENESS**

Scripture: Be kind and merciful, and forgive others, just as God forgave you because of Christ. (Ephesians 4:32)

Preparation: a spray bottle of new car smell

Here's the Talk

Several years ago, someone came up with the idea of marketing a scent called "new car smell." The idea was, since there were many other aromas that one could spray in a car—peppermint, apple, cherry—why not the scent of a new car? A person could have a ten-year-old truck, spray a little new car scent inside it, and wham!—new truck! Many people think the scent of a new car is one of the most pleasing aromas inside an automobile.

Like cars, a friendship can grow stale also. Sometimes a friendship needs a new start. Sometimes people need to forgive each other, make up, or say, "I'm sorry." Without forgiveness and reconciliation, no friendship will last long.

As Christians we have an even better reason to forgive a friend. Since Jesus has forgiven us, we can follow this same example and forgive others.

#35: SUNTAN LOTION FRIENDSHIP

Themes: HELPFULNESS, GENEROSITY

Scripture: If you want to be great, you must be the servant of all the others. (Matthew 20:26)

Preparation: a bottle of sunscreen or suntan lotion

Here's the Talk

How many of you have ever tried to rub sunscreen on your own back? It doesn't work very well, does it?

When we stop to consider all of the things we cannot do by ourselves, the list might astound us. Practically every day, there are things that other people do for us—serve our food in a restaurant, clean our clothes, drive us to school. We need other people.

Friends are people who help each other. Yes, it may be something as simple as rubbing sunscreen onto a friend's back. Without that kind of help, we are likely to get burned. Or friendship may take on even greater qualities, like being there for a friend who is depressed or lonely, doing things together, or helping each other with homework. Jesus went a step further and said that if we are going to be a true friend, we must serve others. Greatness comes not from being served, but from serving.

It is also true that friends are people who confide in each other. When we are hurting, it is important to tell a friend about our feelings. A friend can't know our need unless we talk about it. Good friends communicate with each other.

When you think about being a friend, how do you rate? Are you the kind of friend who is always willing to help? Are you a good communicator? Do you have a servant's heart?

#36: THE JEWEL OF FRIENDSHIP

Themes: INTEGRITY, SINCERITY

Scripture: Don't get tired of helping others. You will be rewarded when the time is right, if you don't give up. (Galatians 6:9)

Preparation: a diamond or other precious stone

Here's the Talk

During the age of the railroad, Diamond Jim Brady was known as one of the most extravagant Americans alive. He would travel around the country for nine months at a time gambling and throwing parties. Diamond Jim got his name because of his jewel collection, which was said to have totaled more than twenty thousand diamonds. Included in this collection were twenty-one complete sets of diamond-studded cuff links, scarf pins, rings, and shirt studs.

Diamond Jim was also known as a voracious eater. For breakfast alone he often ate steak and eggs, chops and pancakes, potatoes, and corn muffins. Brady was known to have ordered fifteen-course meals and top off the evening with all-night dancing. Although Diamond Jim was always surrounded by many people who loved to be in his presence, few actually knew him well, and he had no true friends. Eventually Diamond Jim ate himself to death, suffering a massive heart attack while reclining in his $1,000-a-week high-rise apartment. The year was 1917, and Diamond Jim was sixty-one years old. Diamond Jim lived "the fast life" on the outside. But on the inside, he was lonely.

How fortunate you are if you have friends who love *you* and appreciate *you*! That is the true gem of life. Friendship is worth far more than silver, gold, or precious jewels. When you and I have the treasure of friendship, we are truly rich!

#37: FAMILIAR DISCOVERIES

Theme: JOY

Scripture: Finally, my dear friends, be glad that you belong to the Lord. (Philippians 3:1)

Preparation: an ice cube

Here's the Talk

No human being has stood on the surface of the moon since 1972. For twenty-two years scientists had regarded the moon as a barren hunk of rock and had given up on trying to establish an outpost or lunar base on the surface. That is, until 1994, when lunar probe *Clementine* spotted something odd inside a dark crater on the moon's south pole. This large crater, which sunlight never touches, is more than seven miles deep and has a temperature which does not rise above 380 degrees below zero Fahrenheit. That's cold!

Inside this crater, scientists think they have discovered a patch of ice—probably left behind when a comet crashed into the lunar surface—which is more than twenty-five feet thick. This discovery has led many scientists to regard the moon as a viable place to establish a space post—since water could be obtained there. As it turns out, the moon still has some surprises after all.

Isn't that the way it is with friendship? There is always more to learn about each other. Even if we have known someone a long time, there are still wonderful discoveries to be made in life.

#38: THE GIFT OF FRIENDSHIP

Theme: SACRIFICE

Scripture: Love is always supportive, loyal, hopeful, and trusting. Love never fails! (1 Corinthians 13:7)

Preparation: none

Here's the Talk

There is a Jewish legend about two friends who happened to be farmers. These two men loved each other very much and were always so helpful and kind regardless of the circumstances.

One year there was a terrible famine in the land. Both of the farmers lost their entire crop and were beginning to be in want. One evening, the first farmer thought about the plight of his friend. "I should take him a sack of grain from my storage bin," he thought. "After all, I had a good crop last year and my friend could use the grain for his family." So that evening, in order to spare his friend any embarrassment, the first farmer took a sack of grain from his own bin and, under the cloak of darkness, placed the sack in his friend's barn.

The next morning, however, the first farmer was surprised to find that the sack of grain had been replaced. "God has blessed me," he said. "Because of my generosity and love for my friend, God has seen fit to give me another sack of grain." That evening, and for several evenings thereafter, the first farmer took another sack of grain to his friend's barn. But each morning, he would awake to find that the sack had been replaced.

Night after night this continued until one evening, the first farmer happened to meet the second farmer coming down the road carrying a sack of grain. At that moment they realized that they had been exchanging sacks of grain and ran to embrace each another.

#39: TOUGH TIMERS

Themes: PERSEVERANCE, LOYALTY

Scripture: A friend is always a friend. (Proverbs 17:17)

Preparation: a belt

Here's the Talk

Have you ever stopped to consider how marvelous an invention a belt is? Chances are many of us use a belt every day. A belt is simple, just a strip of leather or cloth, but the function it performs—holding up our pants—is important! We rarely stop to think about a belt; we don't even know that it's there. A belt just does its thing.

Good friends are like that, too. They are always there. Always supportive. Always useful.

In the Book of Proverbs we can find many wonderful passages of wisdom pertaining to friendship. Proverbs 16:28 says, "Gossip is no good! It causes hard feelings and comes between friends." Proverbs 18:24 says, "Some friends don't help, but a true friend is closer than your own family." Proverbs 27:6 says, "You can trust a friend who corrects you."

(*To close this talk on friendship, divide the teens into smaller groups and ask them to reflect on these passages or to look up other Scripture references to* friends *and* friendship *with a concordance.*)

#40: GENTLE SPIRITS

Themes: **GENTLENESS, PATIENCE**

Scripture: Controlling your temper is better than being a hero who captures a city. (Proverbs 16:32)

Preparation: a match

Here's the Talk

(As you begin this talk, light a match.)

Many of us probably know someone we would call a hothead. You know, the one who gets angry the minute something doesn't go her way. But, as the proverb points out, those who are able to control their anger, and vent it properly, are truly strong.

Anger is one of the most useful emotions we can feel. Without ever venting anger, we would all be pent-up time bombs, ready to go off at any moment. But anger which is released in destructive or harsh tones always does more harm than good.

Good friends are able to express anger with each other and still be friends. Friends can disagree and still be friends. Friends don't have to be angry at each other for very long; they can always make up.

A spirit of gentleness and peace is the most wonderful quality we can demonstrate in life. When others are going off like rockets around us, we can still be calm and in control. After all, we know the Prince of Peace, and kindness never goes out of style.

CHAPTER FIVE

OUTDOOR YOUTH TALKS

#41: ROCK OF AGES

Theme: GOD'S STRENGTH

Scripture: You [Lord God] are my mighty rock, my fortress, my protector, the rock where I am safe, my shield. (Psalm 18:2)

Preparation: a rock

Here's the Talk

Many mountain climbing enthusiasts regard the Nabisco Wall in Yosemite, California, as one of the most difficult climbs in the United States. This rock was first climbed in 1973 and takes several days to ascend, due in large part to several vertical patches of mountain face.

The steepest climb in the world is perhaps the Trango Tower in northern Pakistan. Here, rising above a giant glacier that sweeps through the mountain pass, a 3,000-foot spike of granite challenges even the most accomplished of climbers. To ascend this rock, climbers must invest a month or more, and the ascent is often made more harrowing by high-altitude winds and storms that plague the region. Climbers must cook, eat, and sleep in hanging tents secured to the vertical face of the mountain. Now that's a steep rock!

One of the most common metaphors for God in the Scriptures is the image of God as a rock. "You are my rock, my fortress," the psalmist writes, "the rock where I am safe." Rock, of course, is the most common substance on earth—namely because the earth is a rock. So it is easy to see why God is often called an unmoving, unchanging mountain. God's strength and presence can be depended upon. You and I can rest assured that, even though the earth should move and tremble, God will never change nor forsake us.

#42: HEAVENLY SUNSHINE

Theme: ETERNITY

Scripture: The heavens keep telling the wonders of God. (Psalm 19:1)

Preparation: a telescope

Here's the Talk

On July 4, 1997, a spacecraft landed on Mars. This spacecraft, called *Pathfinder*, roved the surface of the red planet, analyzed samples of rock and soil, and contained a camera that enabled scientists to view the terrain and atmosphere. Compared to Earth, Mars is nearly one half the size, but contains some startling features.

For example, scientists believe that Mars contains the largest volcano in our solar system. The giant volcano, known as Olympus Mons, is three times as tall as Mount Everest, the tallest peak on Earth. The crater of this volcano is nearly fifty miles across and is 3,200 feet deep. The volcano itself is so large, more than 435 miles across, and 16.8 miles high, that it must be a sight to behold!

There is also a canyon on Mars, known as the Valles Marineris, which would dwarf the Grand Canyon. This huge canyon would actually stretch the length of the United States—from coast to coast—and is 23,000 feet deep, a depth that would swallow the entire Rocky Mountain range!

Looking through a telescope, we cannot see all of these amazing features on the red planet, but we can see the immensity and astonishing vastness of the universe. Human beings have always been in awe of the creation. The Psalms attest to the fact that people have stood beneath the stars at night and gazed into the heavens, marveling at the great power of the Creator. "The heavens keep telling the wonders of God," the psalmist said. And they are still proclaiming. Thanks be to God.

#43: CREEPY CRAWLERS

Themes: WONDER, AWE

Scripture: God said, "I command the earth to give life to all kinds of tame animals, wild animals, and reptiles." (Genesis 1:24)

Preparation: a bug or other small animal

Here's the Talk

If you've ever been to a zoo or museum, you know there are millions of kinds of animals, insects, and other creeping things that infest the earth. Some of these creatures are most amazing when you stop to look at them closely.

For example, there is a giant beetle—the Goliath beetle—in central Africa that weighs as much as thirty-three pennies. This fearsome-looking insect has a giant horn on its head that is strong enough to peel a banana; it can dig into tree bark to enable the beetle to lap up tree sap. How would you like to have that bug in your bed?

There is also a frog found in the Amazon known as the paradoxical frog. The amazing thing about this frog is that the babies are bigger than the adults! How is such a thing possible? Well, if you remember your biology, you know that tadpoles grow into frogs. The tadpoles start out being seven to ten inches in length, but as they get older, they begin to actually shrink in size and, when they turn into frogs, their hearts shrink in size also. Strange? Yes. But true.

What an amazing world we live in. We have not even begun to fathom the mysteries of life and the wonders of God. But aren't we blessed to live in such a beautiful and varied world?

#44: THE BEACH HOUSE

Themes: WISDOM, FAITH

Scripture: … a foolish person who built a house on sand. (Matthew 7:26)

Preparation: a handful of sand

Here's the Talk

Jesus once told a parable about two people: a wise person and a foolish one. The wise person built a house on a foundation of stone. The foolish person built a house on a foundation of sand. When a storm came and the winds blew upon the houses, the wise person's home withstood the tempest. The foolish person's house, however, since it was built upon the shifting sand, tumbled to the ground when the winds blew against it.

There are many foundations we can build our lives upon. We can build upon those values and teachings that will last forever and withstand any storm of life, or we can build our existence upon the latest fads, the newest trends, or the coolest gimmicks. None of these, however, will last very long. They will not support us when the harshest tests of life come along.

Build your life around the things of God, and you will find a foundation for the future. You can be assured that, no matter what life throws at you, God will be like a rock to you.

#45: CHARGE UP!

Theme: EXCITEMENT

Scripture: Those who trust the LORD will find new strength. (Isaiah 40:31)

Preparation: a rechargeable battery

Here's the Talk

There was once a prophet named Ezekiel who had a vision. In this vision he saw a valley of dry bones—very dry bones. But when the Spirit of God blew across the bones, they began to come together, bone upon bone, and rattle. They stood upright, gained flesh and blood, and began to walk again.

Have you ever felt dry inside? Have you ever needed a new surge of God's Spirit?

Sometimes we become like run-down and depleted batteries. We need new energy, new life. But when we wait upon the Lord, we often find a new zest for life. It is in the waiting that we often find God's strength—not in the doing. Wait. Pray. Seek the Lord. And see if God does not give you a fresh start.

#46: CLEAN LIVING

Themes: CREATION, ECOLOGY

Scripture: God said, "I command the earth to produce all kinds of plants." (Genesis 1:11)

Preparation: a bottle of shampoo

Here's the Talk

Many advertisements for shampoo make extravagant or humorous claims. "Makes your hair feel like a spring rain." "Refreshes while it cleanses." "Moisturizes and cures split ends." "Gently conditions damaged hair—and smells nice, too!"

More and more today, there is an awareness that nature is being damaged and polluted. It will take far more than a bottle of shampoo to clean things up. However, many teens are making a difference. One group of students in Georgia cleaned up a local park. A youth group from Indiana traveled to Louisiana on a mission trip, helping salvage several acres of wildlife refuge while they repaired houses and cleaned up yards.

We don't have to make extravagant claims for our efforts, but we can make a difference. What might we do here in our area to make a difference to the environment?

#47: THE COURAGE TO BE

Themes: TRANQUILITY, PEACE

Scripture: You [God] lead me to streams of peaceful water. (Psalm 23:2)

Preparation: none

Here's the Talk

A famous theologian in the 1960's named Paul Tillich authored a book called *The Courage to Be*. This little volume speaks to the condition of many people living in a hurried and busy age. We find it difficult to relax without having a television on. Even in elevators we are bombarded by music and noise. Some people surround themselves with cellular phones, beepers, pagers, e-mail, and teleconferences. They want other people to have access to them twenty-four hours a day. They can be reached at any time, by anyone.

When we live like this, we rarely find a still moment. Tranquility eludes us. Peace is difficult to obtain. Perhaps you have already begun to feel the pressures of never being alone, of having to fill up your calendar with busy activities and other "stuff." Maybe you long for a quiet afternoon or a peaceful morning, without any distractions or hurried shuffling of papers.

The psalmist reminds us that peace is a gift from God. Finding tranquility comes when we have the courage to *be*, rather than always having to *become*. In our society, we are driven to excel and to make something of ourselves. God says we are already someone—we are God's children. We don't have to prove anything to God. We can just be the people God has uniquely created us to be. How does that kind of peace sound to you?

#48: WHAT'S INSIDE?

Themes: DATING, RELATIONSHIPS

Scripture: I will point out the road that you should follow. (Psalm 32:8)

Preparation: a periodic table of the elements (chemistry)

Here's the Talk

Many students dread chemistry, perhaps because of the periodic table of the elements. At first glance it appears overwhelming. Students wonder if they will be able to memorize it all.

Chemistry is the study of the basic components of the universe: carbon and oxygen, nitrogen and hydrogen—all the stuff of life. It seems amazing that we could all be composed of the same elements and require the same elements to function properly.

Even though we are all composed of the same elements, we know there is far more to a person than atoms. We have feelings, memories, spirit, personality, love, and hope. What makes us human are these unseen qualities. For example, when you go out on a date, you may have a good first impression. But when you look more closely at the person, you may find that he or she has some unattractive qualities. Or you may want to date someone because he or she is good-looking, but find the person unappealing on the inside.

Knowing a person takes time and attention. To love someone, we must look past the outside and see what is on the inside. The inner elements are most important for a relationship. When two people find that these inner qualities are compatible, love takes root and grows.

The next time you are on a date, consider the chemistry of your relationship. What do you see on the inside? What do others see inside you?

#49: PROMISES, PROMISES

Themes: GOD'S PROMISES, VISION

Scripture: I will bless you and give you such a large family ... more numerous than the stars in the sky or the grains of sand along the beach. (Genesis 22:17)

Preparation: a beach towel

Here's the Talk

Did you know that one of the first promises recorded in the Bible was made to Abraham and Sarah, two people who were very old and without children? God promised them many descendants and told them that their family would be as numerous as the sand on the seashore.

You and I are living proof of this promise. We are Abraham and Sarah's children; you and I are the promise that God made to them.

God told Abraham and Sarah, "I will bless you to be a blessing to others." You and I are blessed with this same promise. We can be a blessing to others, too. Through our words and actions, others can know the promises of God, which are as numerous as the sands of the sea.

#50: HAVE YOU HUGGED YOURSELF TODAY?

Theme: SELF-ESTEEM

Scripture: I praise you for the wonderful way you made me. (Psalm 139:14)

Preparation: a leaf or, in winter, a snowflake

Here's the Talk

Nature is filled with uniqueness and wonder. Take a leaf for instance (*or a snowflake*). No two are exactly the same. Likewise, you and I are uniquely created. This may seem obvious to us, but it has some deep implications.

For example, if we believe that God made us, why would we not rejoice in this fact? God made you and me! Our differences are what make the world a fascinating place. Can you imagine how boring the world would be if there were only one kind of tree or one kind of animal or one kind of flower? Boring! God has made many shapes and sizes of people, and many colors. We all reflect the image and majesty of God.

Rejoice! You have been made by God. It's all right to love yourself!

CHAPTER SIX

GAMES YOUTH TALKS

#51: THE MEASURE OF SUCCESS

Themes: OVERCOMING OBSTACLES, COOPERATION

Scripture: We should be patient with the Lord's followers whose faith is weak. (Romans 15:1)

Preparation: a tape measure

Here's the Talk

When Willye White went to the 1956 Olympic games in Melbourne, Australia, she nearly came home with a gold medal in the long jump. Her silver medal in this event inspired her to try again for the gold at the 1964 Olympics in Tokyo. Again she brought home a silver medal in the long jump.

Today Willye White is using her athletic talents to teach children the true meaning of competition and the art of personal achievement. Each day she meets children on the outdoor track at the University of Chicago and teaches them how to run, jump, and cooperate with each other on the athletic field. Although many of the children who come to the program have witnessed violent crimes and are at-risk students in the schools, many find the encouragement needed to turn their lives around.

The measure of success does not always go to the one who can jump or vault the highest or the farthest. Sometimes the greatest success stories are those that happen in people's lives. Willye White sees her work among the poor as a ministry. She is an athlete making a difference to others. Although Willye White never won a gold medal in Olympic competition, she feels that she has won a gold medal in life.

How are you going to measure your success in life? Will it be by athletic accomplishments or trophies? Or will your success story involve the people you helped and the difference you made in a hurting world?

#52: RADICAL RELAY

Theme: HELPFULNESS

Scripture: Your desire to tell the good news about peace should be like shoes on your feet. (Ephesians 6:15)

Preparation: athletic shoes

Here's the Talk

(This is a good talk to use before or after a relay race.)

Have you ever considered what a relay race is all about? It is an attempt to pass something along to someone else.

Although we may not recognize them as such, there are many relays in life, for there are many things that we are passing along to others every day. Some people, for example, pass along a cheerful spirit wherever they go—a smile here, a kind word there. Others pass along negativity and destruction—anger, addiction, violent behavior that leads to more violence. Every word, every act, is a kind of relay. We are passing these attitudes along to others.

Have you ever stopped to think about all of the positive things you have received from others? They have relayed to you positive values, faith, the assurance of God's love in your life. There was a time when we knew nothing of these things. Others had to teach us, relay this knowledge to us.

Jesus asked his disciples to participate in a radical relay of the Spirit. "Pass along this faith," he said. "Tell others the good news. Let your light shine. Be an example of love, as I have taught you."

Each day, wherever we walk or run, wherever we play or study, we can relay something of this message of God's love in the attitudes we have and the kindness we show. Your relay does make a difference. God says so.

#53: TEACHER TAG

Theme: HUMILITY

Scripture: Care about [others] as much as you care about yourselves. (Philippians 2:4)

Preparation: none

Here's the Talk

Sarah Trillin teaches at South Central's Crenshaw High School in Los Angeles. When she first began teaching there, the students she encountered were hesitant to trust or accept her. In an area where many of the students had been exposed to crime and death, many of the students had difficulty seeing a bright future for themselves.

Sarah Trillin set out to change that attitude by giving students respect and asking for their respect in return. In time, she noticed many changes in her students. Some gained a renewed energy for learning. Others were great students but just needed some direction and additional coaching. Although she did influence most of the students who passed through her classroom, she was able to help a handful to turn their lives for the better. She was not able to succeed in all that she did, but there were enough successes to keep her going.

Life is that way, too. Sometimes we need a sense of humility so we will not believe too highly in ourselves. It is acceptable to fail.

Having a sense of humility is often difficult—especially when we are in the classroom or are competing with others. Humility is a trait that is learned. It takes practice and confidence to believe in one's self, and to trust that it is acceptable to fail. Even in competition, humility has its place. Striving is far more important than winning or losing.

#54: WINNERS AND LOSERS?

Theme: GOD'S GRACE

Scripture: But many who are now first will be last, and many who are last will be first. (Matthew 19:30)

Preparation: blue award ribbons for everyone in the group

Here's the Talk

One of the defining moments of a game is when the final whistle blows. The winners rejoice and the losers walk away dejected. We have been taught that this is what the game is all about—winning or losing. There are first place winners and last place losers.

Jesus, however, told his disciples that the kingdom of God is not like this at all. The first would be last, he told them. The last would end up in first place. What is going on here?

The word is *grace*. Grace turns the world upside-down. When God chooses to give grace to someone, it doesn't matter how high up in the standings that person has finished when the final whistle blows. That person has won. That person is in first place.

You see, in God's kingdom, there are no winners or losers—there is not second and third place. There is only first place. God says, "I give you a blue ribbon. You win!"

(*Pass out the blue ribbons, giving one to everyone.*) Take this ribbon home and put in on your wall. You have already won. Because of what Jesus did for you, you are a champion!

#55: SOLITAIRE

Themes: SELF-ESTEEM, REST, RECREATION

Scripture: My dear friends, stand firm and don't be shaken. Always keep busy working for the Lord. (1 Corinthians 15:58)

Preparation: a deck of cards

Here's the Talk

One of the most popular card games of all time is solitaire. There are many versions of this solitary pursuit, but most of us have one or two games that we enjoy playing when we are alone. Solitaire has become so popular that many computers are programmed with solitaire games.

When we are alone, we often have time to think about who we are, what we are doing, and what we hope to become. People do a lot of daydreaming when they are alone or when they play solitaire —maybe that is why the game is so popular. We all need time to think. But finding this kind of solitude can be challenging. Sometimes people are alone because they are lonely or depressed. Some find it difficult to interact with others. And still other people suffer from low self-esteem.

Being alone, however, doesn't have to be a lonely venture. When we realize that God has created us with the need for love, nurture, and care, we can begin to understand that we need rest as well. And our rest comes from God and is a gift of God. You and I need to be re-created each day with down time and recuperation. We need the peace of God.

Take heart! God loves you! You are special. God has given you life and offers you true rest. Being alone with God can be the greatest rest of all.

#56: STRESSED FOR SUCCESS

Theme: STRESS

Scripture: I don't run without a goal. (1 Corinthians 9:26)

Preparation: a certificate of achievement

Here's the Talk

All of his life Mark Lambert wanted to get to the top in the business world. After graduating from high school, he earned a degree in business and soon landed a middle management job at a bank near Chicago. He worked hard. Kept a fast pace. Soon he was rewarded with a top position in the bank's upper management. A few years later, after more hard work, Mark Lambert found himself sitting at the top of the heap as CEO of the bank.

But Mark Lambert was empty inside. After all his years of climbing and scratching to get to the top, he found that the years of stress had eaten away at his soul. He had no heart, no core to his life. He felt hollow.

Setting out to change himself, Mark began to pray every day on his drive to work. Soon he discovered that his attitude was different in the workplace; he treated others with more kindness and gentleness and they, in turn, passed along the goodwill to others. Gradually, the entire company changed.

Mark Lambert, who had always had a dream of playing a professional sport, soon began talking to young athletes in high schools and colleges. He told them about his drive for success and what it had done to him. He reminded them that life is far more than competition. Getting to the top is not the ultimate goal. Living and loving well is the ultimate goal. Life is not a game, it is an adventure.

Where is the adventure of life taking you? Have you opened your life to God's leading, allowing God to remove your stress for success?

#57: FAITH FOUNDATION

Theme: FAITH

Scripture: Christ is the only foundation. Whatever we build on that foundation will be tested by fire on the day of judgment. (1 Corinthians 3:11)

Preparation: a piece of basketball flooring or football turf

Here's the Talk

In the movie *Rudy*—a true story about a young man's quest to make the Notre Dame football team—there is a moving scene where Rudy is talking to a caretaker who is painting lines on the football field. In the background, many other caretakers are scrambling about the field, spraying the turf, manicuring the lawn to perfection before the big game. All of the caretakers are serious about their work. There is a feeling of expectation before game day.

The next day, when the players run out of the tunnel for the game, the cameras pan back and give the audience a full view of the playing field. It is pristine, a lush green surface lined with perfect white lines.

This scene lasts only a few seconds, but it is an important scene in the movie because it emphasizes in a subtle way the invaluable work of the caretaker who helps Rudy get his big chance to play on the field. Without the field itself, there could be no football. Without the foundation, there could be no game.

Did you know that Jesus Christ is the foundation of our faith? Jesus makes everything else possible. Without his work to build upon, we would have nothing. He is the caretaker, the one who makes it possible for us to strive, to grow, to achieve. Whenever we step back and take in the big picture, we see how much Christ has done for us. With Christ, all things are possible.

#58: PRIZED POSSESSIONS

Theme: VALUES

Scripture: Do you not know that in a race the runners all compete, but only one receives the prize? (1 Corinthians 9:24)

Preparation: a runner's baton

Here's the Talk

What do you value most in life? What do you want to pass along to others? What would you classify as your most prized possession?

The next time you watch a relay race on television, take note of the passing of the baton. That small stick is vital to the success of the run. Without a smooth passing of the baton—one runner handing off the baton to another—there can be no victory lap. Winning depends upon the successful passing of the baton.

Every day you and I are passing values and attitudes along to others. We pass along the best things of life, or the worst. We make that kind of a difference to the people we meet, and not only to our friends, but to complete strangers as well.

God has given you an opportunity to pass a baton to someone else. What does your baton represent? How are you passing it along?

#59: DISQUALIFICATION

Theme: DRUGS

Scripture: I punish my body and enslave it, so that after proclaiming to others I myself should not be disqualified. (1 Corinthians 9:27)

Preparation: a red disqualification flag for soccer

Here's the Talk

In the game of soccer, players can be given a yellow flag as a warning for unsportsmanlike play or for personal fouls. If a player gets two of these yellow flags, he or she can receive a red flag, which represents disqualification. The player must sit on the bench for the rest of the game.

You and I hear a great deal about other kinds of disqualification, too. Some people take themselves out of the game of life by being careless and reckless. Their lives end in tragedy. Others make mistakes by turning to violence. Still other people disqualify themselves by using drugs.

Long ago the apostle Paul said that he enslaved his body so he would not be disqualified when it came to the things of God. Subduing our desires and cravings is probably the most difficult aspect of life. Learning how to master our desires requires discipline and faith. Just like an athlete in training, we try to condition ourselves to live well for God and others. All that takes from our conditioning defeats our aim, destroys our purpose.

Live well. Grow in grace. And call upon God for strength in every time of testing.

#60: RECORD BOOK

Theme: SALVATION

Scripture: Another book was opened, the book of life.
(Revelation 20:12)

Preparation: a book of world records

Here's the Talk

Among the strangest records in the world are those for eating. Did you know that, according to the *Guiness Book of World Records*, one fellow ate sixty-three bananas in ten minutes? Another fellow once ate twenty-seven doughnuts in seven minutes, sixteen seconds.

How would you like to meet the fellow who holds the world record for eel eating: 1,300 slimy eels in forty-three seconds? Or the guy who swallowed 500 oysters in an hour? Or the guy who ate 130 prunes in 105 seconds? These kinds of records are as hard to swallow as they are unbelievable. It is amazing to realize that records are kept for most everything in life—even the oddest and strangest of endeavors.

Records may come and go in life, but God will never forget the faithful. God's remembrance of the faithful is often referred to in the Bible as the book of life. This record is one that will never pass away—it is God's gift of salvation. And you and I can trust that God will never forget us.

CHAPTER SEVEN

MISSION TRIP YOUTH TALKS

#61: CHOCOLATE BOX DISCIPLES

Theme: SERVING OTHERS

Scripture: Later the Lord chose seventy-two other followers and sent them out two by two to every town and village where he was about to go. (Luke 10:1)

Preparation: a box of chocolates and (if possible) a video clip of the movie *Forrest Gump*

Here's the Talk

(Begin by showing the clip at the beginning of the movie where Forrest says, "Mama always said, 'Life is like a box of chocolates.'")

In this movie we hear Forrest saying that life is mysterious and uncertain. We never know what tomorrow will bring. And this is certainly true as we go forth to serve others on this mission trip. We do not know whose lives we will touch.

Long ago, Jesus sent out seventy-two disciples to do his work. These men and women went into the villages to heal the sick, help the poor, and proclaim that God's kingdom was near. They did not know what they would find or whom they would help. But they went anyway. Just like us. Being a servant to others is never an easy task. Going on this mission trip involves sacrifice and commitment. We have to step out in faith, believing that God will bless our efforts and our work. Even if we are afraid. (*Pause to ask the teens to name some of their fears about the mission.*)

All of us have fears, but these will not keep us from doing good for others. We can know that God is already preparing the way for us, even when we don't know what tomorrow will bring. (*Pass the chocolates for each to take one.*)

Let's eat a chocolate and remember that our efforts will help others when we allow God to guide us. We can help make someone's life a little bit sweeter, too.

#62: TASTE TEST

Theme: **SERVING OTHERS**

Scripture: You are like salt for everyone on earth. But if the salt no longer tastes like salt, how can you make food salty? All it is good for is to be thrown out and walked on. (Matthew 5:13)

Preparation: several cups of different-flavored drinks and one cup of salt water

Here's the Talk

Perhaps you have seen those commercials where someone undergoes the taste test for a new product. A woman is blindfolded, given two drinks, and asked to choose the one she likes best. Or a man with a cold is given two medicines and is asked to choose the one that cleared up his stuffy nose. Taste tests have been around for a long time. They have been used to promote soft drinks, coffees, diet drinks, and cough syrups. I'd like for all of you to take a silent taste test right now. (*Allow time for everyone to taste a few of the assorted flavors, including the salt water, in complete silence.*)

Who can tell me which of the cups had the (*orange, grape, cherry, or others*) flavoring? Which one did you like the best? Which one had the strongest flavor? (*Someone will mention the salt water.*)

There is no way we can miss salt water when we taste it. Salt, in fact, is one of the most overpowering tastes. Salt has a punch, a kick. That's why we like peanuts and popcorn, pretzels and potato chips. And that's why Jesus told the people that they were to be like the salt of the earth. Jesus wants us to have some power and punch to our lives. We are to give flavor to the world. Like salt on bland food, we can make things better.

Our mission excursion can be a means of making the world a better place. When God uses us, other people know that something powerful is happening. They can't miss it. God's love shines through. And that is our greatest mission of all—to make God's love real to others.

#63: THE POWER OF LOVE

Theme: HOLY SPIRIT

Scripture: Christ also brought you the truth, which is the good news about how you can be saved. You put your faith in Christ and were given the promised Holy Spirit to show that you belong to God. (Ephesians 1:13)

Preparation: a computer floppy disk

Here's the Talk

One thing all of us take for granted is new technology. Especially computers. I can't tell you how a computer works or what is inside the machine that makes all the electronic parts work together. All I know is that when I stick a floppy disk inside the machine and press a key, digitized information is transferred onto the magnetic disk inside the floppy. Whenever I want to retrieve the information, it is there.

A floppy disk serves as a kind of storage unit. And somehow the information is sealed inside the disk, so that it's always there when I need it.

I think that's what this Scripture passage is about. You and I have the promised Holy Spirit in our lives. We have the power of God when we need it. This power is always there, even if we can't see it or explain it.

As we get ready to go on our mission trip, don't forget that you have within you this promise of God—the Holy Spirit. You will be able to do more, be more, and help more than you ever imagined. This is because God lives within you through the Spirit. And it is not your power that is important, but the power which God gives to each Christian.

#64: LICENSE TO LOVE

Theme: CONFIDENCE

Scripture: Such a large crowd of witnesses is all around us! So we must get rid of everything that slows us down, especially the sin that just won't let go. And we must be determined to run the race that is ahead of us. (Hebrews 12:1-2)

Preparation: a driver's license

Here's the Talk

Earning your driver's license was, I'm sure, one of the exciting milestones in your lives. And some of you are looking forward to that moment when you can place your own driver's license in your wallet or purse—when you can say, "I can now drive a car." You look forward to that moment, work for it, study for it, and cherish it when it finally arrives.

Consider what a driver's license is all about. It is a document issued by the state, which says: "We have confidence in you. We believe you have the skill, qualifications, and intelligence necessary to drive a car on public roads."

Think about that. Others have confidence in you. They trust you. You! Driving a car is a privilege, not a right. And there are many people who have helped you accomplish your goal. You did not earn your license by yourself. Others helped you. At every step along the way, other people—from parents, to coaches, to driving instructors, to teachers, to friends—believed in you. They said, "You can do it!"

Did you know Jesus has confidence in you, too? He says, "I believe in you. Your faith is enough. And if you have faith, you can accomplish anything!" This is true. You and I can accomplish much when we work together, when we look to Jesus to complete our faith. We can do great things when we have a common mission, a common goal. God has given us each a driver's license to be his disciples. Let's make the most of it.

#65: HAMBURGER HELPERS

Theme: COOPERATION

Scripture: The body of Christ has many different parts, just as any other body does. (1 Corinthians 12:12)

Preparation: a hamburger with all the works

Here's the Talk

Whenever we think about getting a hamburger, we don't just think about the bun or the pickles or the ketchup, mustard, or special sauce. We aren't just thinking about the beef patty itself. We have a picture in our minds of this thing we call a hamburger. The bun, the patty, the pickles—everything together makes up the hamburger. (*Open the bun and begin removing the lettuce, tomato, pickles, and other condiments.*)

A hamburger is composed of all these tasty items. When you order a hamburger, you don't want it to be lacking any of the individual parts. None of us would ever order a hamburger without a bun. And we usually want lots of extras on the burger.

As you and I prepare to go on our mission trip, it is important to remember that we need to cooperate with each other, we need to work together. Each of us is important to the whole mission. The better we work together, the more we will accomplish and the greater our witness will be.

If we fail to cooperate, that would be like trying to make a hamburger without a bun, a piece of lettuce, or ketchup. We are all individual parts of a whole. All of us together make a team. And this team we call the body of Christ.

#66: THIS OLD COAT

Themes: OUTREACH, LOVE

Scripture: Whenever you did it for any of my people, no matter how unimportant they seemed, you did it for me. (Matthew 25:40)

Preparation: an old winter coat

Here's the Talk

Clothing is something that most of us take for granted. In fact, we probably have far more clothing than we really need. And many of us probably have more than one winter coat.

Long ago, Jesus told a story about some disciples who fed the hungry, clothed the needy, and healed the sick. But these disciples did not realize the impact they were having for the kingdom of God. Jesus said, "When I was hungry, you gave me something to eat, and when I was thirsty, you gave me something to eat. Whenever you did it for any of my people, no matter how unimportant they seemed, you did it for me" (Matthew 25:35, 40).

Being disciples of Jesus, we are often not aware of the good that we do. Being a disciple is never easy, but when we serve others simply and humbly, Jesus says we are serving him. Everyone has something to offer to others, and the good news is that we can do it in the name of Jesus. (*Challenge the teens to bring in an old coat from home as part of their mission trip offering.*)

Prayer:
Lord, as we go to serve you in others, direct our minds and hands and hearts in love. All that we do, we do for you. Amen.

#67: WHAT TIME IS IT?

Themes: STEWARDSHIP; DOING GOD'S WILL

Scripture: These are evil times, so make every minute count. (Ephesians 5:16)

Preparation: an alarm clock

Here's the Talk

Have you ever felt rushed to complete a test at school? Or how about at home, when you are trying to finish a few chores so you can go out with your friends? All of us realize we must live within the confines of time. But we also experience the pressures of time. (*Hold up the alarm clock as you read the Scripture passage.*)

This Scripture passage tells us that God desires for us to make the most of our days. We only have so much time to do good, only so much time to help others. In fact, how we use our time is just as important as how we use our money or talents. God desires that we set aside some time each day for others, to get outside of ourselves and realize that the world does not revolve around our own needs and desires. Jesus lived for others. As his disciples, we are called to live for others, too.

As we go on this mission trip, let's ask God to help us use time to our best advantage. Let's not waste time, but use it wisely. After all, we may never get another chance like this to serve others together.

(*Close the talk by setting off the alarm and offering prayers for the mission effort.*)

#68: PAINT BY THE NUMBERS

Theme: SERVICE, TEAMWORK

Scripture: Work hard at whatever you do. (Ecclesiastes 9:10)

Preparation: a can of paint and brush

Here's the Talk

When most of us think about going on a mission trip, we think about pounding nails on a roof or pouring cement or serving up meals in a soup kitchen. Or maybe we think about slapping a coat of paint on an old wall (*hold up the paint and brush*).

Indeed, our mission trip may require that we do all these things and more. But more importantly, we have an opportunity to show others the quality of our love and the depth of our commitment to Christ. We can demonstrate this love by working well—by doing a good job at whatever we do and by doing it with all our might. We can demonstrate our love for Christ by caring for each other, by being kind and considerate and cooperative. Others will see this in us and will know that we are Christians by our love.

So before you pick up a paint brush or a can of paint, stop to think about why we are doing this work, and pause to remember that we are a team of people who care about each other. That is the greatest work of all. And if we do that, our work will truly be a blessing to others.

#69: LOVE POTION

Themes: CARING, SERVICE

Scripture: People judge others by what they look like, but I [the Lord] judge people by what is in their hearts. (1 Samuel 16:7)

Preparation: a spray bottle of cologne

Here's the Talk

Let's be honest—we live in a society that is infatuated with beauty and good looks. Most of us spend inordinate amounts of time trying to look good. We even like to smell good. (*Spray some of the cologne into the air and let the aroma settle upon the group. Or pick out a few volunteers and let them sample various perfumes.*)

A long time ago, there was a young man named David who was, shall we say, thin and lanky, a bit uncoordinated, and the youngest in the family. He was a typical teenager. And he probably had zits too! But, in spite of his outward appearance, David was chosen by God to become king of Israel. God told the prophet Samuel, "People judge others by what they look like, but I judge people by what is in their hearts."

As we go to serve others, let's all take a shot of love potion with us. This is not a perfume that can be purchased in any store and, in fact, you can't even smell it. But you can see it! It's an attitude of love that exists in all who follow Jesus. We see the difference it makes when we realize that our work for the kingdom of God is far more important than any string of pearls or diamond earrings. People look on the outward appearance, but God looks at our hearts.

What is in your heart? Are you filled with a love for Christ and others? Is that why you want to serve on this mission team? I hope so! We can all stand a little of that love potion.

#70: KEY RING FAITH

Themes: **FAITH, HOPE**

Scripture: I will give you the keys to the kingdom of heaven, and God in heaven will allow whatever you allow on earth. But he will not allow anything that you don't allow. (Matthew 16:19)

Preparation: a key ring

Here's the Talk

(*As you begin the talk, invite the youth to show their various key rings or chains to others in the group.*)

You know something—a key ring is valuable, isn't it? If we lost our keys, we wouldn't be able to start our cars, get into our homes, or open our lockers. Most of us keep careful tabs on where our keys are at all times, and we probably have a place where we put our keys when we are not using them.

Long ago, Jesus gave Peter "the keys to the kingdom of heaven." I think Jesus was talking about faith, about working to make the kingdom come to earth as it is in heaven. This is an important set of keys! Jesus told Peter that he could unlock heaven and earth with this faith. Wow!

As we go on our mission trip, I hope we will keep our hearts and minds focused on all the right things. Let's not misplace our keys and have to go looking for them. Without faith, our mission work will be hollow and may not get off to a good start. Without faith we will be searching for the key that will unlock our joy, hope, and care for others. Keep the key of faith on your key ring as we go on this mission trip. And who knows, we might even be making a difference in heaven as much as we are on earth.

(*Close by inviting the teens to rattle their keys as a sign of their anticipation and willingness to assume the work of faith.*)

CHAPTER EIGHT

SPORTS YOUTH TALKS

#71: Reaching for the Gold

Theme: HAVING A VISION

Scripture: The heavens suddenly opened. The LORD placed his hand upon me and showed me some visions. (Ezekiel 1:2-3)

Preparation: the Olympic logo, or a gold medal or athletic award

Here's the Talk

During the years that Billy Payne played football for the University of Georgia, he would ask his father after every game, "Dad, how did I do?" And his father would reply, "Son, did you do your best?" Billy Payne, for some reason, could never answer this question. But he knew he wanted to do something that would enable him to say, "I did my best!"

Years later, after Billy Payne had graduated from college and had become a successful real estate attorney in Atlanta, he and his family were driving home from church one Sunday. The pastor had challenged the people to have a vision, to celebrate something bigger and grander than themselves. He told his wife, "I need a new dream."

That next year, Billy Payne got involved in leading his congregation in a new building program. But he didn't stop there. He wanted something for the entire city of Atlanta, in fact, the entire country. With the help of a few friends, he set out to bring the Olympic games to Atlanta. Billy Payne was not only able to say he had done his best, but he was also able to say he had a new vision. He had dreamed a dream and made it a reality.

What are your dreams today? for yourself? for our youth group? What can we do together that would enable us to say, "We have done our best"?

#72: CHRISTIAN CALISTHENICS

Themes: GOD'S STRENGTH, FAITHFULNESS

Scripture: God is wonderful and glorious. I pray that his Spirit will make you become strong followers. (Ephesians 3:16)

Preparation: none

Here's the Talk

(Before the talk, invite the students to do as many sit-ups, push-ups, or jumping jacks as possible. When everyone is tired, gather the group in a circle and begin.)

At the 1976 summer Olympics, a fourteen-year-old named Nadia Comeneci dominated the women's gymnastics. She won not only two of the individual events, but also won a gold medal as the best all-around women's gymnast. Growing up in Romania, a poor country that had been closed in many respects to the rest of the world, this teenager was able to overcome many adversities. She was able to rise above her circumstances through commitment to her goals and a firm belief in herself.

As you can see, being a top athlete requires great strength and dedication. Without proper training, we quickly tire. The same is true in life. Without God's strength to uphold us, we would quickly wither and die. God's strength and power make it possible for us to live well, to love well, and to overcome the greatest adversities of life. Getting into shape spiritually requires that we plug into God's power and lean upon God for strength and assurance.

#73: THE UNBREAKABLE RECORD

Themes: CREATION, GOD'S POWER

Scripture: In the beginning God created the heavens and the earth. (Genesis 1:1)

Preparation: none

Here's the Talk

Many people who follow professional sports believe there are some records that will never be broken. For example, Wilt Chamberlain once scored one hundred points in a basketball game. Wilt also pulled down fifty-five rebounds in a single game and, over the course of one season, averaged more than fifty points per game.

Likewise, in baseball, Roger Maris hit sixty-one home runs in a season. And Joe DiMaggio hit safely in fifty-six consecutive games. Some believe that these records will stand the test of time and never fall.

But there is one record we know will never be broken. Long ago, God created the heavens and the earth. In other words, God created everything that exists. Think about this achievement! What could be grander? The next time you look up into the skies and count the stars at night or see a field of wildflowers that seem to go on forever, consider all that God has made. Surely God's power is beyond comprehension and his wonders extend to the ends of the universe.

#74: VITAL STATISTICS

Themes: ADORATION OF GOD; PRAISE

Scripture: Keep your minds on whatever is true, pure, right, holy, friendly, and proper. Don't ever stop thinking about what is truly worthwhile and worthy of praise. (Philippians 4:8)

Preparation: a baseball card

Here's the Talk

(Hold up the baseball card and read off a few of the player's statistics before you begin the talk.)

Often, when people talk about sports, they want to know about statistics. How many victories? How many defeats? Who is the tallest? the fastest? the strongest? Statistics are a way of measuring one athlete against another.

Did you know that statistics have been important to Christians, too? That's right. But statistics of a different sort. We should not be concerned about who is the greatest or who is the most talented or who has the most money. Rather, Christians are people who are concerned about doing the greatest good for God—even good that often goes unnoticed and unappreciated.

In this Bible passage, we are asked to focus our minds and efforts on doing what is true, pure, right, holy, friendly, and proper. Even though others may not see these efforts or take note of them, God does. In fact, Jesus once said, "He knows what is done in private, and he will reward you" (Matthew 6:6). This is one of the most difficult aspects of being a Christian. We often want immediate praise and reward; we want others to notice our efforts and our deeds. But what is most important is that God sees what we do. And when we stay focused on the positive, God notes our attitude as well. The most vital statistic of all is what God sees in us.

#75: RULES OF LIFE

Themes: OBEDIENCE, FAITHFULNESS

Scripture: No one wins an athletic contest without obeying the rules. (2 Timothy 2:5)

Preparation: a high school athletic rule book

Here's the Talk

How many of you know the rules of volleyball? basketball? some other sport? How would you go about explaining these rules to someone? *(Allow the youth to attempt to explain their favorite sport to the group.)*

Rules are very important in competition. In fact, when an athlete breaks the rules in order to win, he or she is usually disqualified, and, even worse, looked down upon by the other competitors. No one wants to compete with a cheater. And no one can truly be called a champion who breaks the rules of sportsmanship and fair play.

Life itself is made up of rules, isn't it? What if there were no rules for driving? What if everyone were allowed to choose at random if, or when, he or she wanted to work or go to school or complete a job? Chaos would soon reign. People would die on operating tables if doctors and nurses decided when they would work. In fact, there would be no such thing as society.

Thankfully, God has given us many rules to live by. Some of these rules are difficult to follow, others are simpler. Most of us would never murder or rape anyone, for example. But we might find it difficult to keep from lying or saying hateful words. Even though God has given us these rules, it is difficult to keep them all.

However, when we learn to rely upon God's forgiveness and goodness, we understand that, even though we are not always good, God is! Running the race of life is much easier when we know that God is waiting for us at the finish line with open arms. May the love of God inspire us all to live well, and within the rules God has given.

#76: MOUNTAIN CLIMBING

Themes: PERSEVERANCE, TRUST, COOPERATION

Scripture: Timothy, my child, Christ Jesus is kind, and you must let him make you strong. (2 Timothy 2:1)

Preparation: a backpack

Here's the Talk

In the spring of 1996, several people froze to death near the peak of Mount Everest—the world's tallest mountain, reaching five and a half miles into the atmosphere. The climbers who died were not unprepared to challenge the elements of nature. Nor were they ill-equipped or inexperienced. But, in the thin atmosphere of Everest, their physical strength ran out when a violent storm descended upon the mountain.

There are many items that a mountain climber might carry in a backpack: water, oxygen, extra articles of clothing. But no amount of preparation can overcome exhaustion. Going the distance is difficult in mountain climbing, and it is often difficult to be faithful in each and every situation of life. Sometimes we find ourselves growing weary in the life of discipleship. We want to turn back. We want to give up. In these moments, we are challenged to find our strength in one another and in God.

That is why our group is so important to each of us. We need the strength that we find in our common faith. We need each other's help and love. We need to know that we never walk through life alone. You and I are on a journey. And sometimes it feels like we are climbing a mountain. But isn't it wonderful to know that we can climb it together?

#77: HOT DOG HEAVEN

Themes: **FALSE GODS, SIN**

Scripture: You had wandered away like sheep. Now you have returned to the one who is your shepherd and protector. (1 Peter 2:25)

Preparation: a hot dog with all the works

Here's the Talk

If you have ever gone to a baseball game or a basketball game, perhaps you have noticed that many people spend more time eating than they do watching or participating in the game. There is nothing wrong with eating a hot dog, for instance, but being part of the crowd, participating in the game, is much better. A hot dog may taste good for a little while, but in the end, it doesn't satisfy for very long. Being a participant in the game has a far more lasting impression.

Life is like this, too. Sometimes we get our priorities mixed up. We can put those things that are important to God and others on the periphery of our lives. We can focus all of our energy and effort on things that ultimately don't matter much or for very long.

Let's stay in the game and be faithful to what God has called us to be—disciples of Jesus. Let's stay focused on what is important. And let us try to shield ourselves from those influences that take our hearts and minds off of God and the good of others. One of the greatest challenges in our discipleship is trying to live out God's agenda rather than our own. Having a hot dog heaven may seem satisfying for a time, but in the end we are left wanting the things of God. Let's help each other to stay focused on the things of God instead of those things that do not last.

#78: FOOTBALL FOLLIES

Theme: GOD'S PROTECTION

Scripture: You are my strong shield, and I trust you completely. (Psalm 28:7)

Preparation: a football helmet

Here's the Talk

Years ago, when American football was in its infancy, people played without helmets or protective gear of any kind. Naturally, as the game became more and more physical, there were injuries, many of them serious. Then someone had the brilliant idea of wearing a helmet. Wow! Protection! What a brainstorm!

In the Psalms, which are some of the world's oldest poetry, there are many affirmations and statements of faith about God. One of the most frequent references to the Creator is the image of God as a shield. Imagine, God is our protector. God watches over us and keeps us from harm.

Such an idea may seem simple, but can you imagine going through life without this kind of simple faith? Think of all the times when you have been protected from harm. Consider all those moments when something horrible could have happened to you—but, for some reason, you were unharmed. That is what the Psalmist is trying to express. You, God, are my strong shield, and I trust you completely.

(Close the talk by inviting the teenagers to repeat this verse and hopefully to memorize it.)

#79: "FAN"ATICISM

Themes: FRIENDSHIP, LEADERSHIP

Scripture: Such a large crowd of witnesses is all around us! So we must get rid of everything that slows us down, especially the sin that just won't let go. And we must be determined to run the race that is ahead of us. (Hebrews 12:1)

Preparation: a ticket stub to a sporting event

Here's the Talk

Did you know that the word *fan* is derived from the word *fanatic*? It's a fact. Sometimes we even call sports fans *fanatics*. A ticket will get you into a sporting event, but it will not necessarily make you a fan. Being a fan means that you follow your team closely, you know the players by name, and you are eager to see your team win.

Did you know that, every day of our lives, we are surrounded by many unseen fans who are cheering for us? Sometimes these fans are called "the great cloud of witnesses"—all the followers of Jesus who have come before us. We have them as our example and our inspiration. With this great cloud of witnesses behind us, cheering us on, we have every reason to believe that we can complete our race of faith. We will arrive at our heavenly destination, too.

As the writer of Hebrews suggests, running a race to the very finish requires perseverance and stamina. Our race is not a short sprint but a long distance run. Keep going, the writer is saying. Don't give up. Other people have already blazed the trail. They have shown the way. They are the great cloud of witnesses.

#80: THE SIGN IN THE GRANDSTAND

Theme: GOD'S LOVE

Scripture: God loved the people of this world so much that he gave his only Son, so that everyone who has faith in him will have eternal life and never really die. (John 3:16)

Preparation: a large sign with "John 3:16" written on it

Here's the Talk

Back in the late 1970's and early 1980's there was a fellow who appeared on television at most of the major sporting events. He could often be seen wearing a rainbow-colored wig, holding up a large sign with the words "John 3:16" written on it. This fellow was seen so much, in fact, that he became known as "Mister John 3:16."

John 3:16, as you may know, is one of the most often-quoted verses in the entire Bible. (*Hold up the sign and quote the verse now.*)

There have been many, like Mister John 3:16, who believe that this verse summarizes the gospel message. It is the good news of Jesus in a nutshell: God loves the world; God wanted to give to the world; and so God gave an only son—Jesus—to be the savior of the world; those who believe in him will never, never, never die.

This message is simple, but very powerful. More people have embraced this message, and believed in it, than any other message in the history of the world. You and I believe, too. And we can help to spread this message each day. Oh, we don't have to make a sign and go on television to have an impact on people. We can show this love of God to others. We can proclaim this message by living in a loving relationship with God, by speaking the truth, and by telling others that Jesus loves them. Who knows? You and I might be the only example of God's love that another person will ever see.

#81: JOY TO THE WORLD

Theme: CHRISTMAS

Scripture: Don't be afraid! I have good news for you, which will make everyone happy. (Luke 2:10)

Preparation: a musical instrument

Here's the Talk

In early 1860, a pastor in London began a work among the poor of London's East Side. This area was filled with slums and great poverty. Although the work was difficult, the pastor attempted to meet the needs by appealing to churches. Few responded with help or financial assistance.

Not dismayed, the pastor decided to take his work to the streets. He organized small instrumental bands, started a newsletter, and worked directly with the poor. These instrumental bands, composed of trumpets, trombones, horns, and flutes, often played songs on the street corners and asked for donations. People responded. As a result, a movement was born that has made an impact on many people at Christmas time.

The pastor was William Booth, and he founded a church called the Salvation Army.

Today many people are familiar with the Salvation Army shield and the sound of bells ringing outside of stores, beckoning busy shoppers to consider the poor and needy. William Booth wanted others to remember that the joy of Christmas was to be shared with the whole world and that the spirit of Christmas could be a year-round undertaking.

There is an old saying: Christmas is not a season—it is an attitude. Yes, and when we live with that spirit of Christmas in our hearts all year long, there is truly a joy to the world.

#82: COUNTING THE DAYS

Theme: CHRISTMAS

Scripture: About that time Emperor Augustus gave orders for the names of all people be listed in record books. (Luke 2:1)

Preparation: a calendar or electronic organizer

Here's the Talk

People who pay taxes quarterly keep a close eye on the calendar. Payments are due in January, April, June, and September. You can be sure that many people have these dates memorized, and they might even dread to see them approaching.

Long ago, the emperor of the Roman world, a man named Caesar Augustus, ordered everyone to return to his home town to pay a tax. It was during this time that Jesus was born to Mary and Joseph.

Even though it may seem strange, God does everything at the right time. From our perspective, it doesn't seem like the perfect time for a Messiah to be born—there was no world-wide television or radio to record the event. It took a long time for people to get the good news of Jesus' birth. But in God's timing such things are irrelevant.

God does everything at the appropriate time. Sometimes we become impatient when things do not happen quickly enough to suit our desires. Often this causes us to place our trust in things rather than God.

God will do everything at the right time in our lives too. We can trust that all things will work together for us when we love God. Although we cannot put God's time in our calendars or electronic organizers, we can trust that God will make a way for us too—in God's good time.

#83: THE GREATEST GIFT OF ALL

Theme: EPIPHANY

Scripture: They took out their gifts of gold, frankincense, and myrrh and gave them to him. (Matthew 2:11)

Preparation: a twig

Here's the Talk

Leo Buscaglia, a noted author, told a wonderful story about a particular gift he received one year from the Christmas angel. Leo was just a boy and had not been particularly good. In Italian tradition, it was the Christmas angel, not Santa, who brought the gifts to little girls and boys, and Leo was particularly anxious to see what the angel would put in his stocking.

Can you imagine how little Leo felt when, opening his stocking, he found that it had been filled with nothing but a dry twig? He was heartbroken. All of his brothers and sisters had received fruits and other goodies. They were elated. But why had the angel given him nothing but a twig? The answer came when Leo's mother explained, "You see, Leo, this is what happens to little boys who are bad. The Christmas angel sees everything!" Leo fell into his mother's arms, sobbing.

Soon all of his brothers and sisters were sobbing too. They began to share their goodies with Leo. Soon he had as much as anyone in the family.

The greatest gift of the magi was not the gold or precious ointments they brought to the Christ child, but their spirit of giving. This is the greatest gift of all. When you and I learn to share with others, we have learned the true spirit of Epiphany—that of giving. Epiphany is the season where we celebrate this spirit of giving—God's gift to the whole world—the gift of Jesus.

#84: GOD'S LEFTOVERS

Theme: LENT, COMMUNION

Scripture: This is my body, which is given for you. Eat this as a way of remembering me! (Luke 22:19)

Preparation: Communion elements or bits of bread

Here's the Talk

Chances are, everyone here has eaten leftovers at one time or another. When it's late at night and we get hungry, we often go to the fridge for a cold slice of pie and some ice cream, or maybe there is a stale donut hanging around in the bread drawer. Many people eat leftovers on the weekends. And there are many people who think that some foods—like chili, soup, lasagna, and stews—get better with age. The longer they sit around in the refrigerator, the better they taste.

Leftovers have been around for a long time. Jesus himself even used leftovers.

After Jesus had celebrated a final Passover meal with his disciples in a small upper room, the gospels tell us that Jesus took some bread that was leftover from the supper. This was bread that had already been broken, passed around several times, and nibbled on. He told the disciples, "This is my body, broken for you."

After supper, Jesus took a cup of leftover wine—a cup that had been raised in celebration at least three times during the Passover meal. This wine had already been sipped and enjoyed, but Jesus said, "This is my blood poured out for you and many for the forgiveness of sin."

When you and I partake of the Lord's Supper, or Communion, we are actually eating God's leftovers. God can take what no one would want and make something wonderful and beautiful. That is the power of God. Jesus gave a small piece of bread and a leftover cup of wine to his disciples to remind them, "I am with you always."

#85: THE POWER OF THE CROSS

Theme: LENT, GOOD FRIDAY

Scripture: It was about nine o'clock in the morning when they nailed him to the cross. (Mark 15:25)

Preparation: a pocket cross

Here's the Talk

I am going to ask you to play a game of word association with me. I ask that you close your eyes. In a moment I will say a word. When I say the word, I want you to remember the first image that pops into your mind. Are you ready? (*Wait until all of the teenagers close their eyes.*)

POWER!

Now open your eyes. What image did you see? Some of you may have seen a giant generator turning and spinning with electrical energy. Perhaps some of you saw a desk in a room in the White House with a seal of authority hanging on one wall. Others may have seen a finger poised over a glowing red button. And some of you may have envisioned a baseball player slugging a home run. Those are all images of power.

But the Scriptures tell us that the cross of Jesus has a power unlike any other. Jesus said, when he was lifted up on the cross, he would draw all people to himself (John 12:32). That's power! The apostle Paul said that the cross seems foolish to many people, but to those who have salvation, it represents the power of God (1 Corinthians 1:18). That's power!

You see, the cross is not a good luck charm or a piece of jewelry. The cross is God's way of giving redemption to the world. The cross of Jesus is a gift of life. It is a gift of hope. The cross tells us that, no matter how difficult life gets—and even if we suffer to the point of death—God will never forsake us. There is hope in suffering. There is nothing that can separate us from the love of God in Christ.

#86: NOBODY HOME

Theme: RESURRECTION, EASTER

Scripture: Jesus isn't here! He has been raised from death. (Luke 24:5)

Preparation: an empty box with a top

Here's the Talk

(Begin this talk by inviting one of the teens to reach into the box. Prepare him or her to reach into the box by saying the following.)

I have here a valuable prize. If you reach inside the box, and feel around, you can have whatever is inside. This may be one of the greatest prizes you will ever receive. (*Allow the youth to reach into the box without looking inside. The youth will soon discover that the box was empty.*)

What did you find inside? Nothing? How do you feel about that as a prize?

Did you know that Christians celebrate Easter because something was empty? Christians believe that the greatest prize we could ever receive is an empty tomb. When the disciples ran to the tomb, they discovered that there was nothing inside. They also received word, "He is not here. He is risen!" Easter is the most joyous day of the year, but Easter can take place every day of our lives. When we realize that nothing, not even the power of death, can claim us, that is the greatest prize of all.

#87: LONELY HEARTS

Theme: VALENTINE'S DAY

Scripture: I pray that the Lord will guide you to be as loving as God and as patient as Christ. (2 Thessalonians 3:5)

Preparation: a valentine card

Here's the Talk

Many of you probably have been giving and receiving valentine cards since you were children. Valentine's Day is one of the most popular days to express love and care for others. Some of you might even make your own valentines, or perhaps you write a special letter to someone you care about very much. Even though Valentine's Day is not a Christian holiday, it is a great time to let others know that you care about them.

But have you ever stopped to think about all the people who may not receive valentines? People in prison, in nursing care facilities, or who have no family or friends may feel very lonely on Valentine's Day.

This year when you are buying or making a valentine for that special someone, why not take the time to make a valentine for someone you know who is lonely? Send that person your card. You might give that person one of the greatest expressions of God's love they have ever received.

#88: WIND STORM!

Themes: THE HOLY SPIRIT, PENTECOST

Scripture: Suddenly there was a noise from heaven like the sound of a mighty wind! It filled the house where they were meeting. (Acts 2:2)

Preparation: an electric fan

Here's the Talk

(Before you begin your talk, turn the electric fan on and aim it at the group.)

Can you imagine what the world would be like without wind? The trees would never move—neither would the air and clouds. We would never be able to see flowing grain in the fields or feel the sea breeze upon our faces at the beach. We would not be able to enjoy the aroma of flowers or witness so many other beautiful acts of nature. Without wind, the world would be an unmoving, stagnant place.

Most of us would probably not associate the Holy Spirit with wind, but the word for *spirit* and *wind* are actually the same in Greek. Spirit has to do with movement—with power and feeling. When the Holy Spirit is present, things happen!

Like the wind itself, we cannot see the Holy Spirit. But like the wind, we can see the effects of the Holy Spirit on others. If I were to turn this fan on high, we could see the effects it would have on our hair. We could feel the cooling effect on our faces. Likewise, when the Holy Spirit is active and present among us, we can see this in the lives of others, and can feel the warmth and love of God in our midst.

Pentecost is not something that happened long ago. Pentecost can happen every day of our lives—when we open our hearts to the power of God's Spirit.

#89: BACK-TO-SCHOOL BASICS

Themes: GROWTH, LEARNING

Scripture: Love should always make us tell the truth. Then we will grow in every way and be more like Christ, the head of the body. (Ephesians 4:15)

Preparation: a high school class syllabus

Here's the Talk

Have you ever heard of the "Three R's"? I'll bet your parents have. Long ago, teachers used to stress the "Three R's" in school: "Readin', 'Ritin', and 'Rithmatic." These subjects, just like today, were considered to be basic components of a well-rounded education.

Basics are important in everything we do. If you wish to play basketball, for example, the coach will stress the importance of learning to dribble, pass, shoot, and play defense. If these basics are not mastered, a player will lack the skills to play well. Or if you choose to play a musical instrument, it stands to reason that you will have to master the basic fingering and notes before progressing to the more advanced levels.

Going back to school reminds us that learning is important, not just when we are teens but throughout life. Today most businesses have recognized the importance of sending employees to continuing education events. New discoveries and techniques are being developed all the time. No one can afford *not* to learn. So take advantage of these opportunities when you are young. Learn as much as you can now, while your mind is fresh and alive and you are full of new ideas and dreams.

Also, as you go back to school, concentrate on what is truly important. Seek to learn as much about God as you can. Your knowledge of the things of God will serve you well no matter what you do or where you go in the future.

#90: THE MASK FACTOR

Themes: HALLOWEEN, ALL SAINTS' DAY

Scripture: This king won't judge by appearances or listen to rumors. (Isaiah 11:3)

Preparation: various Halloween masks

Here's the Talk

Halloween, or All Hallow's Eve, is more than just a time for trick or treat. It is also a time when the church, traditionally, remembers those who have died within the community of faith. Masks originated years ago when people had festivals to make fun of death, to laugh at the bad things that can happen to us in life. Laughing at these horrible things helped people face their fears and overcome them.

Halloween may be a time of wearing masks, but many people wear masks every day. They pretend to be one type of person when in reality they are someone else. We sometimes call such people hypocrites. The word *hypocrite* comes from a Greek word meaning, "to have two masks."

Human beings can fool one another, but God knows the true heart of everyone. We don't have to pretend to be something we are not. We are free to be ourselves. We can wear a mask of gentleness and kindness, and other people will say that is how we truly are. We can be loving and caring, and others will know that we are truthful. God sees us as we are. Without masks. This is the most wonderful kind of freedom we can know.

CHAPTER TEN

MORE YOUTH TALKS

#91: A GOOD NAME

Themes: GOODNESS, RESPECT

Scripture: A good reputation and respect are worth much more than silver and gold. (Proverbs 22:1)

Preparation: an autograph of a famous person

Here's the Talk

The Declaration of Independence contains some of the most famous autographs in American history. Today, many people collect autographs of celebrities, athletes, and authors. It seems that getting an autograph is one way for people to prove to friends and relatives that they have actually met a famous individual.

But having a famous name and having a good name are often two different things. Some people are famous, have great wealth and fortune, but are not highly respected by others. In fact, it is sometimes their bad reputation that makes them famous. They are known for being difficult, nasty, and unpleasant.

This proverb reminds us that making a good name for ourselves is far greater than obtaining great wealth or fame. If others think highly of us, that is one of the most important accomplishments of life—and one of the most difficult. Your autograph and mine may never be highly valued or prized, but the quality of our friendship will long be remembered by those who love us and know us best.

#92: PADLOCK PRAYERS

Theme: PRAYER

Scripture: When you pray, go into a room alone and close the door. Pray to your Father in private. He knows what is done in private, and he will reward you. (Matthew 6:6)

Preparation: a padlock for a locker

Here's the Talk

Sometime in school you have probably been given a padlock for a locker. Or maybe you have a locker at school where you keep your books and other private things. What you keep inside a locker can be special, maybe even quite meaningful to you—pictures of friends and family, love letters, favorite books.

Jesus talked about having a place where we could express our private concerns to God. He said that God sees what we do in secret and knows our needs even before we express them.

You see, prayer doesn't have to be a public or open expression. Prayer can be very private, a conversation between you and God. You might even think of your prayer as being under lock and key. Only you and God know what is inside.

#93: THE MARK OF CHRIST

Theme: ASSURANCE

Scripture: This is my new agreement: "The time will come when I, the Lord, will write my laws on their minds and hearts. I will be their God, and they will be my people." (Hebrews 8:10)

Preparation: a temporary tattoo

Here's the Talk

Several years ago there was a Canadian tattoo artist, "Sailor Joe" Simmons, who had an amazing 4,831 tattoos on his body. This fellow appeared in many magazines and shows in the 1960's and became the epitome of the image of the "tattooed sailor."

Today many people get tattoos as a form of permanent decoration or art. Some do it for the shock value. Others to impress a boyfriend or a girlfriend. Some even do it as a mark of prestige. And, in certain circles, tattoos are signs of gang activity, of belonging to a certain gang or group.

You and I are part of a group, too. We call it the church. But we do not have to get a tattoo or other physical marks to show others that we are part of God's family. Rather, God has written the new covenant on our minds and hearts. God's marks distinguish us by our actions and our attitudes. God's marks are spiritual marks, not a physical mark, which God has given to all those who love and follow the savior.

#94: TIME PASSAGES

Themes: MEMORIES, FRIENDSHIP

Scripture: Good people are remembered long after they are gone. (Proverbs 10:7)

Preparation: a high school yearbook

Here's the Talk

(To get the talk started, tell the group a few of your high school highlights and allow them to see some of the pictures of your favorite memories in the yearbook.)

One of the most common words in the Bible is *remember*. When the Israelites crossed the Jordan into the Promised Land, they were asked to remember their suffering in Egypt and their time of hardship in the wilderness. When the prophets spoke to the people, they asked them to remember the orphan and the widow. When Jesus gave the disciples a bit of bread and a cup of wine, he asked them to eat and drink in his memory.

In many ways, our lives are collective memories. Without these memories we would have no identity, no past. We would have no history to draw upon for strength and knowledge.

The memories you make in high school will be important ones for you. In them you will find many friendships and strong ties that will deepen your faith and give you confidence for the future. Cherish these memories and friendships. Write about them. And continue to grow wise in the ways that will lead you closer to God.

#95: CHOICES

Themes: DISCERNMENT; WISDOM

Scripture: If you have good sense, instruction will help you to have even better sense. (Proverbs 9:9)

Preparation: a *TV Guide*

Here's the Talk

D.W. Griffith is considered by many to be the father of modern cinematography. He was the first movie producer and director to use such special effects as close-ups; and in one early movie he had more than sixteen thousand extras on the set to film a spectacular scene. Even though Griffith had a few early successes, however, he made many bad choices later on. Most of his later movies were financial flops, and fewer and fewer people wanted to see his films. Eventually Griffith turned to alcohol. He had two marriages that fell apart. Finally, after moving to New York, Griffith was unable to complete his autobiography and was unable to produce any of the plays he had written for the Broadway stage. He died in a hotel lobby from a massive hemorrhage in July, 1948, just as Hollywood movies were entering the golden age of cinema.

Movies and television, and the people who produce the shows we watch, are replete with tragic stories as well as successful ones. But life, just like the movies, is full of drama and difficult choices. Some of our choices can lead to a satisfying life, others to disappointment and disillusionment. Wisdom is knowing the difference between these good and bad choices. Have you ever made any choices you have regretted? What difficult choices have you made that have made you proud?

#96: ReTURN TO OZ

Theme: APPRECIATION

Scripture: Honesty will keep you safe. (Proverbs 28:18)

Preparation: a movie ticket (or, if you prefer, a video of *The Wizard of Oz*)

Here's the Talk

One of the most popular movies of all time is *The Wizard of Oz*. It is the story of Dorothy and her dog, Toto, who find themselves, after flying through a tornado, in the land of the Munchkins. In this strange land, Dorothy meets several interesting characters: a scarecrow who wants a brain, a tin man who wants a heart, and a cowardly lion who desires courage. Dorothy and Toto want to get back to Kansas. Together they travel to the distant city of Oz to seek the wisdom of the great wizard. But the wizard tells them they must prove their worthiness by bringing him the broom of the wicked witch.

Through a series of hair-raising events, Dorothy and her friends do manage to destroy the witch and bring her broom to the wizard—only to discover that the great and powerful wizard of Oz is none other than a silly old man. At the end of this scene, however, the wizard gives everyone what they were yearning for. Of course, by this time, all of the characters have what they were wanting anyway. The scarecrow receives a diploma—even though he has been the brains of the outfit through the entire movie. The lion receives a certificate of courage—even though he had already shown courage by pursuing and helping destroy the witch. And the tin man receives his heart—even though he was always the most emotional of the characters.

When the tin man receives his heart, the wizard tells him, "The quality of love is not so much measured by how much you love, but by how much you are loved by others."

If other people love you, you are indeed very rich. When people sense that you have integrity, that you are true to your values and character, they will love you for who you are.

#97: CAR WARS

Themes: JEALOUSY, ENVY

Scripture: Selfish people cause trouble, but you will live a full life if you trust the LORD. (Proverbs 28:25)

Preparation: car keys, or a picture of a nice car

Here's the Talk

A young man pulled his souped-up car into the school parking lot on his first day at the new school and was greeted by a crowd of other students eager to get a peek at the beautiful automobile. Everyone seemed visibly impressed except for one young man who kept pacing around the car and offering remarks each time he passed.

"This is the ugliest piece of junk I've ever seen," he told the new student as he walked by the first time. As he rounded again he offered a second observation, "No girl in school would be caught dead in this bucket of bolts." Finally, after a third time round the car, he offered another disparaging remark, "You've got to be the nerdiest guy in school this year."

Another student came over, put his arm around the young man and said to him, "Don't pay any attention to anything that guy says. He's nothing but a busybody, a loafer, and a gossip. All he does all day long is go around repeating what he hears other people say!"

Jealousy often comes out in many different forms. Sometimes we even tear others down when they have something we do not. Jealousy and envy are difficult emotions to let go of. They can consume us.

But when we are secure with ourselves, confident of our own abilities and proud of what we have and what we have accomplished, jealousy and envy have no way to take root in our hearts. What accomplishments give you the most pride?

#98: SHOW ME THE MONEY!

Themes: MONEY, GREED

Scripture: But more than anything else, put God's work first and do what he wants. The other things will be yours as well. (Matthew 6:33)

Preparation: a fifty or one hundred dollar bill

Here's the Talk

Perhaps we have heard the phrase "money is the root of all evil." Some people interpret this to mean that money itself is a bad thing, but such is not the case. Money can do many good things as well as bad.

There is a story about a millionaire who wanted to donate some money to a church, but the congregation refused to accept the money because they said it was "tainted" by the bad reputation of the giver. Mother Teresa of Calcutta caught wind of this and immediately called the millionaire, asking for his donation for the poor. He agreed, and gave! When word of this got back to the church, many people were critical of Mother Teresa. But she responded by saying she would gladly take any money, even if it was "tainted," and would transform it with the power to do good.

If we look closely at the world around us, we can see many positive things made possible by money. Without donations of money, many schools and hospitals would be unable to function. Thousands of not-for-profit organizations would be forced to close. A great many charities would grind to a halt—including the church!

You and I live in a society that craves money. We see examples of greed every day. And yet, somehow, generosity is greater! Jesus asked that we not worry about tomorrow. He said God would provide for us. When we have this type of generosity, we find that together there is always enough for everyone.

#99: WORRY WARTS

Theme: WORRY

Scripture: Can worry make you live longer? (Matthew 6:27)

Preparation: a pocket calculator

Here's the Talk

A little girl was walking with her grandmother through the woods. "Grandmother," she wanted to know, "what if I meet a nice boy but he doesn't want anything to do with me?" "Give him something nice, like a piece of candy," grandmother answered. "But what if doesn't like candy?" the little girl asked.

"Then write him a note," the grandmother said. "What if he can't read?" the girl asked. "Then sing him a song." Again the little girl asked, "But what if he doesn't like my singing?" Grandmother sighed and offered another suggestion, "Give him a kiss."

"Oh, no!" the little girl responded. "I don't want him to like me that much!"

Have you ever had a bad case of the "What Ifs"? What if this happens? What if that happens? Have you ever worried about something for so long, and lost so much sleep over it, that you never even had to face what you feared? Of course, we all have. That is the nature of worry. We worry about things that we imagine might happen. But reality rarely concedes that life will turn out exactly like our worries.

Jesus asked his disciples not to worry about tomorrow. He said there would be enough real troubles in a day without having to make up imaginary ones. Even if we sat down with a pocket calculator and tried to figure out how long we would live, or how much we will be worth when we die or count down the days we have left, we would never be able to guess a single thing about the future. That is God's domain.

Give your worries to God. Sleep better at night. Tomorrow will take care of itself.

#100: NEVER APART

Theme: GOD'S PRESENCE

Scripture: I will be with you always, even until the end of the world. (Matthew 28:20)

Preparation: a cellular phone

Here's the Talk

In the mid-1970's, several people were taken hostage in Beirut, Lebanon. One of these hostages was Terry Waite, a British negotiator who was taken captive after going to effect the release of several Americans.

During his nearly nine years in captivity, much of it in solitary confinement, Terry Waite was forced to find a strength beyond himself. He began to memorize Scripture, reading over and over a little Bible that his captors had given to him. It was during this terrible ordeal that many of the words of Scripture began to have a deep meaning in his life. They were not just words, but promises of God.

Most of all, he was forced to lean upon the strength and assurance of God. The words of Jesus, "I will be with you always," were particularly meaningful.

You and I rarely have to think about being apart from anyone at any time. We can even take a telephone with us wherever we go—we can always be reached. This is the kind of assurance Jesus wants to give us as well. No matter where we go, or what happens to us, he is there. Jesus is never out of touch or unreachable. As the prophet Jonah prayed from the belly of the great fish, "I had sunk down below the underwater mountains; I knew that forever, I would be a prisoner there. But, you, LORD God, rescued me from that pit" (Jonah 2:6).

SCRIPTURES

SCRIPTURES (CONT.)

THEMES

THEMES (CONT.)